MARTHA COLLISON

pull up a chair

MARTHA COLLISON

pull up a chair

Recipes for Gatherings Big and
Small, from Morning to Night

KYLE BOOKS

For Kenaniah, my sweet son

First published in Great Britain in 2025 by Kyle Books, an imprint of

Octopus Publishing Group Ltd
Carmelite House
50 Victoria Embankment
London EC4Y 0DZ
www.octopusbooks.co.uk
www.octopusbooksusa.com

An Hachette UK Company
www.hachette.co.uk

The authorized representative in the EEA is Hachette Ireland,
8 Castlecourt Centre, Dublin 15, D15 XTP3, Ireland
email: info@hbgi.ie

Copyright © Octopus Publishing Group Ltd 2025
Text copyright © Martha Collison 2025

Distributed in the US by Hachette Book Group
1290 Avenue of the Americas, 4th and 5th Floors
New York, NY 10104

Distributed in Canada by Canadian Manda Group
664 Annette St., Toronto, Ontario, Canada M6S 2C8

All rights reserved. No part of this work may be reproduced or utilized in any form or by any means, electronic or mechanical, including photocopying, recording or by any information storage and retrieval system, without the prior written permission of the publisher.

Martha Collison asserts the moral right to be identified as the author of this work.

ISBN 978-1-80419-242-9

A CIP catalogue record for this book is available from the British Library.

Printed and bound in China.

10 9 8 7 6 5 4 3 2 1

Commissioning Editor: Judith Hannam
Junior Commissioning Editor: Isabel Jessop
Senior Editor: Alex Stetter
Art Directors: Nicky Collings and Jaz Bahra
Designer and Illustrator: Claire Rochford
Photography: India Whiley-Morton
Food styling: Holly Cowgill
Prop styling: Tabitha Hawkins
Senior Production Manager: Katherine Hockley

Contents

6 Welcome to my kitchen

12 Breakfast table

34 Coffee table

58 Squeeze round the table

86 Table for two

108 Picnic table

130 Weekend table

160 A table of delights

188 Drinks trolley

202 Glossary of UK/US terms
203 Index
207 Acknowledgements

Welcome to my kitchen

My kitchen is my happy place – my space to cook and create, to serve up a family feast, bake biscuits for my nieces and nephews, or unwind alone while kneading dough for my favourite loaf of bread. Nothing delights me more than filling my kitchen with plentiful meals or trays of treats, and inviting people – often more than will comfortably fit around the table! – to join me there, gathering every mismatched chair in the house to squeeze everyone in.

I am a loud advocate of maintaining the tradition of eating together. Our family table is the centre of our home, the spot people are drawn to as they come through the door and the place where they congregate. Everyone is welcome and anyone can pull up a chair. Sometimes our table is the focal point of a party, every inch covered with treats, drinks and nibbles, at other times it plays host to a single tray of cookies, ready to share with a cup of tea and a listening ear. When we were looking for our first flat, my stubborn insistence on finding a one-bedroom flat with an open-plan dining space within our tiny budget led to a particularly long search, but we held out and we found one. And I'm so glad we did, as that dining space became the heart of our small home, and it was where we began to practise hospitality in a genuine, meaningful way.

The word 'entertaining' carries connotations of fluster and fussiness, of laying out a crisp tablecloth and popping the cork of a bottle of the best champagne. It conjures up images of spending hours (or days) planning menus and working tirelessly in the kitchen, creating picture-perfect platters designed to impress, so that the beneficiaries of your hospitality will leave filled with tales of your lavish skills, wondering how they will ever be able to repay the favour. But nowadays, we crave authenticity: we want to host in a no-frills, effortless way, and on a regular basis, rather than saving those shared moments for infrequent special occasions. In a world where we juggle tasks and activities, in which convenience seems to be king, there is significance to be found in savouring food with other people. Hosting can be messy, but it is always meaningful. The concept of sharing food and conversation is a simple one, and my aim with this book is to reignite the joy you can find around the table, simply by pulling up a chair.

That chair might be a stool at a breakfast bar, or you might be sitting around a coffee table, or there may be no table at all. On my travels around the world, I've had some of the best conversations and most memorable meals sitting cross-legged on a rug covering a dusty floor, sharing food and stories. We all know that we eat first with our eyes – that's where those picture-perfect platters come in! – but I believe we also eat with our ears, and that the stories we connect to favourite recipes are part of the reason we return to them again and again. There is no greater compliment for an avid cook than the question 'Can I have the recipe?'– the request to relive a moment and pass it on to others, to be savoured over and over again. Sitting and eating together is a celebration of humanity, a brief moment in our busy days when we sit, eat and share our lives.

I truly hope this book is inspiration for you to clear a space at your table and extend an invitation for others to pull up a chair and join in.

Martha x

How to use this book

This book has been designed as a guide to hosting, with chapters focusing on the different moments when you may share a recipe. Some of the recipes are perfect for two, others are an invitation to squeeze in as many people as possible and feed them all a bowl of something delicious. There is a chapter celebrating outdoor eating (think picnics and barbecues), and a chapter of drinks designed to impress. And of course, no good cookbook is complete without recipes for cakes! Two chapters are dedicated to sweet treats, either on the coffee table or in the form of desserts that delight. From breakfast to dinner, I hope you find recipes that tickle your fancy and inspire you to invite friends (and strangers) to pull up a chair in your home.

COOK'S NOTES

I've tried to make the recipes in this book accessible, celebrating both store-cupboard staples and seasonal produce, without too many niche ingredients. Here are a few notes on some of the most commonly used items in my recipes:

Eggs
For baking, I always use large, free-range eggs at room temperature.

Butter
I prefer to use full-fat, salted butter. I only opt for unsalted butter for things like buttercream or hollandaise, where too much salt is overwhelming. Make sure that butter is at the correct temperature for the recipe. I always keep a block of butter at room temperature for baking, and the rest in the fridge for all other cooking.

Sugar
Caster sugar, icing sugar and soft light or dark brown sugar are the ones I use most often in this book. Each type of sugar has a different flavour profile and imparts a different texture, so try to adhere to the specific ones listed, or at least the same general type of sugar, where possible.

Meat and poultry
I'm a big advocate of higher-welfare meat and poultry, as it is not only a better choice ethically, but also in terms of the flavour and texture of the finished dishes. Buy the best meat you can afford, and choose local producers where possible. To ensure a more even cook, let your meat and poultry come to room temperature – about 30 minutes to an hour should be enough – rather than cooking it straight from the fridge.

Oil
My favourite and most frequently used type of oil is olive oil. I opt for extra virgin olive oil for salad dressings and to finish dishes, and choose a milder olive oil for cooking. Vegetable or sunflower oil are best for deep-frying, and sesame oil is another great option to have in your store cupboard, for imparting its nutty flavour to savoury dishes.

Salt
I like to use flaky sea salt to season most dishes, and as a finishing touch before serving. Fine sea salt or table salt is preferable for breads, baking recipes and for seasoning pasta water.

Milk and yogurt
I recommend using whole milk, but semi-skimmed is a suitable alternative, if you prefer it. I always use full-fat dairy products, because low-fat versions often contain sugars or thickeners that can alter the flavour and texture of the finished dish. Greek yogurt is my preference, unless thinned natural yogurt is specified in the recipe.

Herbs and spices
Ground spices and dried herbs you can find in the supermarket are what I've used in this book, but be sure to check that your supply is stored correctly and everything is within its 'best before' date, as spices lose heat and intensity quickly when exposed to air and as they age.

Fruit and vegetables
This book is filled with recipes to take you through the year, with something for each season. Pick recipes that celebrate seasonal produce when it is at its best, and try to buy locally grown fruit and vegetables where possible to maximize freshness and flavour. Frozen or canned versions will work too, but will have a slightly different texture, so be aware of this when making swaps.

Weights and measurements
I emphatically recommend getting hold of some digital scales, as volume measurements and other weighing methods simply won't deliver the same level of accuracy. A set of labelled measuring spoons is also a must, to ensure you're adding the correct quantities. All spoon measures in the recipes are level unless otherwise stated.

A FINAL NOTE ON RECIPES

I am not one to be a stickler for the rules, and so I write recipes to act as a guide, for you to make your own, to suit your own taste. We all have different preferences and tolerances for flavour components, so don't be afraid to adjust the spice levels, or add more salt, sweetness (such as honey, syrup or sugar) and acid (citrus juice or vinegar) where you see fit. I test each recipe thoroughly, but can't account for differences in equipment, cooking styles or ingredients, so use your instincts, taste as you cook and adjust things accordingly. However, when it comes to baking recipes, I recommend sticking as closely to the written recipe as possible, as baking is much more of a science, with carefully balanced ratios required to achieve success. Similarly, all ovens are different, so judge by eye, aroma and feel whether a dish is cooked. I find it helpful to test my oven temperature every once in a while using an oven thermometer placed into the centre of the oven to ensure accurate calibration. All the recipes in this book have been tested using an electric fan-assisted oven.

Breakfast table

Elevate porridge to the next level with this nutty baked oat dish: it is almost like having cake for breakfast! You can swap out the almond butter for peanut butter if you prefer. The oats themselves aren't intensely sweet, so I'd recommend serving with extra honey or maple syrup to drizzle if you've got more of a sweet tooth.

Raspberry almond baked oats

Serves 4–6 ~ Preparation time 20 minutes
Cooking time 40–45 minutes

vegetable oil, for greasing
180g (6oz) rolled oats
300ml (10fl oz) milk (almond or dairy)
4 tablespoons almond butter
2 large eggs
2½ tablespoons runny honey or maple syrup
1½ teaspoon baking powder
pinch of salt
225g (8oz) raspberries
2 tablespoons flaked almonds

1. Preheat the oven to 190°C (170°C fan/375°F/gas mark 5) and grease a medium-sized rectangular or oval ovenproof dish with a small amount of oil.

2. In a large bowl, mix together the oats, milk, almond butter and eggs until they form a smooth batter. Add the honey, baking powder and salt, then beat again until well combined. Set aside for 10 minutes to thicken slightly.

3. Tip the raspberries into the bottom of the oven dish and use a fork to roughly mash them. Spread them out in an even layer, then pour over the batter. Sprinkle the flaked almonds over the top, then bake for 40–45 minutes, or until set and golden brown.

4. Serve hot with dollops of Greek yogurt and extra berries and honey to sweeten, if needed, or allow to cool and slice into squares for breakfast on the go. The portions will keep for up to 5 days in the fridge. They can be eaten cold or reheated.

TIP
Baking this recipe in a large dish makes it great for sharing, but I also love making these baked oats in individual portions to eat throughout the week. Simply divide the berries and mixture between 4 large ramekins and bake as above – they will take 15–20 minutes to cook.

Slightly less sweet than the ones you might find at a coffee shop, these muffins are the perfect addition to your breakfast table. Blood oranges add a beautiful burst of pinkish hue to the top, but regular oranges will do the job just as well.

Blood orange, poppy seed and yogurt muffins

Makes 12 muffins ~ Preparation time 20 minutes
Cooking time 12–14 minutes

100g (3½oz) caster sugar
2 blood oranges (or regular oranges)
120g (4¼oz) plain flour
80g (2¾oz) wholemeal flour
3 tablespoons poppy seeds
1½ teaspoons bicarbonate of soda
½ teaspoon salt
2 large eggs
125g (4½oz) full-fat Greek yogurt
3 tablespoons olive oil

FOR THE TOPPING
2 tablespoons full-fat Greek yogurt
2 tablespoons icing sugar

1. Preheat the oven to 220°C (200°C fan/425°F/gas mark 7) and line a 12-hole muffin tin with muffin cases.

2. Tip the caster sugar into a large mixing bowl. Grate the zest of both oranges and add three-quarters to the sugar, reserving the rest for decoration. Stir to infuse the sugar with the zest.

3. Add the plain and wholemeal flour, poppy seeds, bicarbonate of soda and salt to the zesty sugar and mix well to combine. In a jug, beat together the eggs, yogurt and olive oil. Juice one of the oranges and add it to the jug.

4. Pour the wet ingredients into the dry ingredients and use a spatula to fold them together until just combined – don't overbeat, or you'll end up with tough muffins. Divide the mixture between the muffin cases, filling each around three-quarters full.

5. Slice the peel off the remaining orange, then cut the flesh into thin rounds. Cut each round in half and place a piece on top of each muffin, then bake for 6 minutes before reducing the oven temperature to 190°C (170°C fan/375°F/gas mark 5) and baking for a further 6–8 minutes. A skewer inserted into the centre should come out clean, and the muffins should feel spongy to the touch. Allow to cool completely.

6. In a bowl, beat together the yogurt and icing sugar until smooth, then drizzle or pipe over the cooled muffins. Sprinkle with the reserved orange zest and enjoy! Once decorated, these muffins will keep for up to 3 days in the fridge.

TIP
These muffins freeze well, but I'd recommend doing so without the yogurt topping.

A stained-glass window of colourful roasted fruit to cheer your breakfast right up! Serve hot or cold; it's equally delicious as a topping for creamy porridge in winter or served with thick Greek yogurt in summer.

Honey-roasted fruit

Serves 4–6 as a topping ~ Preparation time 15 minutes
Cooking time 40–45 minutes

2 oranges
½ ripe pineapple
1 white grapefruit
1 pink or red grapefruit
3 tablespoons acacia honey, plus extra to serve
1 tablespoon olive oil

1. Preheat the oven to 220°C (200°C fan/425°F/gas mark 7). Slice the top and bottom off each piece of fruit so it sits flat, then use a sharp knife to carefully remove the skin.

2. Cut the fruit into slices and remove the core from the pineapple. Arrange the fruit slices in a large roasting tin, aiming to create a single layer. Drizzle with the honey and olive oil, then toss well so each piece is coated.

3. Roast for 25 minutes, or until the fruit slices and their juices begin to caramelize, then turn over and bake for a further 15–20 minutes. The cooking liquid will thicken as it cools, so don't worry if it seems watery.

4. Allow to cool slightly before serving warm with yogurt or porridge, and more honey for drizzling. Store any leftovers in a container in the fridge for up to 3 days.

I tend to find blueberries a little lacklustre compared with some of their punchier berry relatives – but cooking them really concentrates their flavour and transforms them into something vibrant. These ricotta pancakes are light yet rich, with a flavour reminiscent of blueberry cheesecake, especially when topped with crumbled biscuits!

Blueberry cheesecake pancakes

Makes 8 pancakes ~ **Preparation time** 15 minutes
Cooking time 4–6 minutes per batch

2 large eggs
250g (9oz) ricotta cheese
125ml (4fl oz) semi-skimmed milk
1 tablespoon caster sugar
100g (3½oz) plain flour
1 teaspoon baking powder
100g (3½oz) blueberries, plus extra to serve
vegetable oil, for frying

TO SERVE
maple syrup, for drizzling
2 digestive biscuits, crumbled
Greek yogurt

1 Separate the eggs, placing the yolks into a large bowl and the whites into a smaller bowl. Add the ricotta and milk to the egg yolks and whisk until smooth.

2 Whip the whites in a separate bowl until they form soft peaks (use an electric whisk, or be vigorous with a balloon whisk), then add the sugar and whisk again until thick and glossy; it should be similar to a meringue mixture.

3 Combine the flour and the baking powder in a third bowl, then sift over the top of the egg and ricotta mixture. Use a whisk to combine, then swap to a spatula and carefully fold the egg whites through the mixture. Try not to overmix – you want the batter to be light and airy. Add the blueberries and fold again.

4 Place a large frying pan over a medium heat and brush with oil. Dollop a few tablespoons of batter into the pan and nudge into a circle – depending on the size of your pan, you should be able cook a few pancakes at a time. Cook for 2–3 minutes on each side until golden brown and cooked through. Repeat with the remaining batter, and keep the pancakes warm in a low oven.

5 Serve piled high, drizzled with maple syrup and topped with crushed biscuits, with yogurt and extra berries on the side.

TIP
Any leftover pancakes will freeze well and can be reheated from frozen in a frying pan or in the toaster.

Is it a pudding? Is it French toast? I don't care how it is described, only that it is delicious! This is a breakfast to make for those you love, perfect for Valentine's Day. It's also a great dish for the food-waste conscious among us, as this is the perfect way to revive croissants that are a little dry and past their best.

Hazelnut croissant bake

Serves 2–4 ~ Preparation time 20 minutes
Cooking time 25–30 minutes

knob of butter, for greasing
4 croissants, ideally slightly stale
75g (2¾oz) chocolate hazelnut spread
2 eggs
250ml (9fl oz) whole milk
1 teaspoon vanilla bean paste
1 tablespoon caster sugar
2 tablespoons chopped roasted hazelnuts (see tip)
fresh berries, to serve

1. Preheat the oven to 200°C (180°C fan/400°F/gas mark 6) and grease a medium-sized baking dish (I like to use an enamel roasting tin) with butter.

2. Use a serrated knife to slice each croissant in half horizontally and spread the insides with a generous amount of hazelnut spread. Sandwich together, then tear or slice each one into three evenly sized pieces.

3. Place the filled croissant pieces in the greased dish and muddle them together into an even layer, overlapping in places.

4. In a measuring jug, beat together the eggs, milk, vanilla bean paste and sugar until smooth. Pour this mixture over the top of the croissants, gently turning them with a spatula so they absorb most of the liquid (they will continue to absorb as they bake, so don't be concerned about any pools of liquid). Leave to sit for 5 minutes, then sprinkle with the hazelnut pieces and bake for 25–30 minutes. The bake should be golden brown and puffed up, and there won't be any liquid remaining. Serve piping hot with fresh berries for a proper breakfast treat!

TIP
Ready-chopped roasted hazelnuts are available at most major supermarkets, but if you can't find them, you can easily make your own. Heat a small frying pan over a low heat and add a small handful of blanched hazelnuts. Cook for 8–10 minutes, shaking the pan often, until the nuts look toasted and smell fragrant. Allow to cool, then roughly chop with a sharp knife.

Spicy, sweet and filling enough to see you through the whole morning! This is a great dish to scale up for a crowd, as the oven does the hard work and all you need is a fried egg per person to finish. I often serve this for dinner too – a versatile recipe to add to your repertoire.

Harissa, sausage and sweet potato oven hash

Serves 4 ~ **Preparation time** 15 minutes
Cooking time 35 minutes

- 1 large sweet potato, chopped into 2cm (¾in) cubes
- 1 red onion, halved and thinly sliced
- 1 yellow pepper, roughly chopped
- 1 tablespoon olive oil, plus extra for frying
- 4 chorizo-style pork sausages
- ½ 400g (14oz) can chickpeas
- 1 tablespoon rose harissa paste
- 4 large eggs
- sea salt flakes and freshly ground black pepper
- chopped chives, to garnish

1. Preheat the oven to 220°C (200°C fan/425°F/gas mark 7) and find a large roasting tin (about 33 x 45cm/13 x 18in) or baking tray. Add the sweet potato cubes to the tin, along with the onion, yellow pepper and olive oil, then toss well to combine. Season with a small pinch of sea salt flakes and a good grinding of black pepper.

2. Tear the sausages into small pieces, and add to the roasting tin. Roast for 20 minutes, then remove from the oven and add the chickpeas and harissa paste. Stir together, tossing everything well until completely coated in the harissa and chorizo juices. Return to the oven for a further 15 minutes, until the sweet potato is tender and the chickpeas are crisp.

3. Just before the end of the cooking time, fry the eggs in a little oil in a frying pan until the whites are set but the yolks are still runny. Divide the hash between 4 bowls, then top with an egg and a sprinkle of chives.

TIP
If you can't find chorizo-style sausages, try using regular sausages and adding 1 teaspoon of smoked paprika to the sweet potatoes. Alternatively, you could use cured chorizo, but you won't need to use as much as it is more intense in flavour.

This recipe came about as a happy accident while I was searching for uses for leftover buttercream. It has all the delicious appeal of French toast, but is much quicker to make. Slathering the brioche with buttercream and introducing it to a hot frying pan creates a delicious caramelized layer that hardens as it cools – a seriously indulgent way to treat your loved ones.

Buttercream brioche toast

Serves 4 ~ Preparation time 10 minutes
Cooking time 20–25 minutes

100g (3½oz) unsalted butter, at room temperature
50g (1¾oz) icing sugar
zest of ½ lemon
8 thick slices of brioche

FOR THE STRAWBERRY SAUCE
250g (9oz) strawberries, sliced, plus extra to serve
1 teaspoon cornflour
25g (1oz) caster sugar
juice of ½ lemon

TO SERVE
chopped pistachios
Greek yogurt

1. To make the strawberry sauce, combine the strawberries, cornflour, sugar and lemon juice in a small saucepan. Place over a low heat and warm through, stirring often, for 5 minutes, or until the berries have softened and are surrounded by a thick sauce. Set aside.

2. In a small bowl, mix together the butter, icing sugar and lemon zest until smooth. Lightly spread this mixture on both sides of each brioche slice.

3. Heat a large nonstick frying pan over a medium heat, then reduce the heat to low and, working in batches, add the buttered brioche slices. Toast very gently for 2–3 minutes on each side until caramelized to a deep toffee-brown colour, then place on a wire rack to set while you fry the rest.

4. When everything is ready, stack a couple of slices of toasted brioche on each plate and top with the strawberry sauce, then scatter with pistachios, Greek yogurt and more strawberries before serving.

TIP
If you happen to have some leftover buttercream to hand, you can skip a step and just use that instead.

Yogurt, chilli butter and eggs might sound like an unusual combination for breakfast, but once you've dunked a piece of toast into this creamy, garlicky sauce flecked with egg yolk, you'll be sold! I love to serve Turkish eggs with parsnip fritters – the sweetness from the vegetables brings the whole dish into balance. If you can't get hold of parsnips or they aren't in season, try replacing them with grated carrot.

Turkish eggs with parsnip fritters

Serves 4 ~ **Preparation time** 20 minutes
Cooking time 30 minutes

FOR THE FRITTERS
3 parsnips, coarsely grated
½ teaspoon ground cumin
½ teaspoon smoked paprika
2 spring onions, finely chopped
2 eggs
vegetable oil, for frying

FOR THE YOGURT
150g (5½oz) full-fat Greek yogurt, at room temperature
1 garlic clove, finely grated
1 tablespoon finely chopped dill
pinch of salt

FOR THE POACHED EGGS
4 fresh eggs
1 tablespoon white wine vinegar (optional)

FOR THE CHILLI BUTTER
75g (2¾oz) salted butter
½ teaspoon smoked paprika
2 teaspoons pul biber, or ½ teaspoon red chilli flakes

TO SERVE
fresh dill
crusty bread

1. Begin by making the fritters. In a large bowl, combine the grated parsnips with the cumin, paprika, spring onions and eggs, then stir well to combine.

2. Add just enough oil to a large frying pan to form a thin layer and place over a medium heat. Once the pan is hot, spoon 3–4 heaped tablespoons of the fritter mix into the pan, pressing them down gently so they cook evenly. Cook for 4–5 minutes on one side, then flip over and repeat on the other side. The fritters should be golden brown and cooked through. Keep warm in a low oven while you fry the remaining fritters, adding a touch more oil as you do so.

3. For the yogurt, combine the Greek yogurt, garlic, dill and a generous pinch of salt in a bowl. Stir well, then set aside.

4. Make the poached eggs. Bring a medium saucepan of water to a simmer and add the vinegar if your eggs aren't very fresh. Crack an egg into a ramekin, then pour it quickly into the water. Repeat with the remaining eggs, then poach for 3–4 minutes or until the whites have set but the yolks are runny. Remove with a slotted spoon to drain.

5. To make the chilli butter, melt the butter, paprika and pul biber flakes in a small saucepan over a medium heat (or use the pan you poached the eggs in, after you've drained it). Cook for 2–4 minutes until foaming, then remove from the heat.

6. Divide the fritters between 4 plates, top with the garlic yogurt and a poached egg each, then pour over the hot butter. Serve with fresh herbs and crusty bread to mop up the sauce and yolk!

Two things guaranteed to get me up in the morning are: the smell of bacon and the smell of coffee. This recipe combines them both: maple-coated bacon with a hint of espresso, and sweet espresso butter that melts all over the thick, fluffy slices of French toast. The espresso butter is great on banana bread, too!

French toast with maple-espresso bacon

Serves 4 ~ Preparation time 20 minutes
Cooking time 20 minutes

175ml (6fl oz) whole milk
2 large eggs
1 teaspoon vanilla extract
1 tablespoon caster sugar
pinch of fine sea salt
4 slices (about 2.5cm/1in thick) challah bread (or other soft white bread), a few days old
40g (1½oz) salted butter

FOR THE ESPRESSO BUTTER
1 teaspoon espresso powder
½ teaspoon boiling water
1 tablespoon icing sugar
60g (2¼oz) salted butter, at room temperature

FOR THE MAPLE-ESPRESSO BACON
2 tablespoons maple syrup, plus extra to serve
2 tablespoons espresso (freshly brewed or made up from espresso powder)
8 smoked streaky bacon rashers

1. To make the espresso butter, dissolve the espresso powder in the measured boiling water in a small bowl, then add the icing sugar. Allow to cool for a few minutes, then add the soft butter and beat well until smooth. Spread on a sheet of baking parchment or clingfilm and pat into a block shape, then refrigerate until needed.

2. To make the maple-espresso bacon, preheat the oven to 200°C (180°C fan/400°F/gas mark 6) and line a baking tray with baking parchment. Combine the maple syrup with the espresso in a small jug. Lay out the smoked streaky bacon on the prepared tray, and use a pastry brush to brush each rasher with the coffee mixture. Bake for 10 minutes until beginning to crisp, then turn over and brush the other side of each rasher with the mixture before baking for a further 10 minutes until crisp. Drain on a sheet of kitchen paper to absorb any excess grease.

3. Meanwhile, beat together the milk, eggs and vanilla extract in a wide rectangular dish that is big enough to hold two pieces of bread. Add the sugar and salt and beat again.

4. Melt half the butter in a large frying or griddle pan over a medium heat. Dip 2 slices of bread into the egg mixture and soak for 15 seconds on each side until saturated.

5. Fry the two soaked bread slices for 3–4 minutes – reducing the heat if necessary – until golden and caramelized on the bottom, then flip over. Cook for a further minute or two on the other side until puffed up and cooked through, then remove from the pan and keep warm in a low oven until ready to serve. Soak the remaining bread slices into the egg mixture, then melt the remaining butter in the pan and fry as before.

6. Serve with the crispy bacon, a cube of espresso butter and more maple syrup if desired.

For a traditional shakshuka, eggs are poached in a spicy tomato sauce. Here I have created a fresh and vibrant brunch dish celebrating green spring vegetables at their finest. Top with tangy feta and spicy jalapeños for a delicious wake-up call.

Green shakshuka

Serves 2 ~ Preparation time 10 minutes
Cooking time 15–20 minutes

2 tablespoons olive oil
1 leek, trimmed and finely sliced
2 garlic cloves, finely chopped
½ teaspoon ground cumin
1 large courgette, finely diced
75g (2¾oz) kale, stalks removed, roughly chopped
juice of 1 lemon
50ml (2fl oz) water
4 eggs
100g (3½oz) feta cheese, crumbled
1 avocado, stoned, peeled and finely sliced
small handful of coriander, finely chopped
1 green jalapeño chilli, finely chopped
sea salt flakes and freshly ground black pepper
buttered sourdough or warm flatbreads, to serve

1. Heat the olive oil in a large frying pan over a medium heat (choose a pan that has a lid). Add the leek and sauté for 3–4 minutes, or until softened. Add the garlic and cumin, followed by the courgette and kale. Cook, stirring often, for a further 4–5 minutes, until the vegetables are tender but still vibrant. Squeeze in the lemon juice and stir in the measured water.

2. Create four small wells in the mixture using the back of a spoon and crack an egg into each well, taking care not to break the yolks. Lightly season the eggs with salt and pepper and reduce the heat to low. Cover with a lid and cook until the egg whites have set – this will take 5–7 minutes.

3. Top with the feta, avocado, coriander and chilli. Serve immediately with buttered sourdough or warm flatbreads.

Eggs Benedict is my go-to order whenever I go out for brunch – I think I may be addicted to hollandaise sauce. I used to think it was too difficult to make at home, but this recipe works every time, especially when you have a few tricks up your sleeve if your sauce splits! Storing the sauce in a Thermos flask once it is ready also takes the pressure off, so there's no need to rush the other elements of your dish.

Crab and avocado eggs Benedict

Serves 2 ~ Preparation time 10 minutes
Cooking time 10 minutes

4 large eggs
150g (5½oz) fresh white crab meat
zest and juice of ½ lemon
4 crumpets (or 2 English muffins, halved)
1 avocado, stoned, peeled and finely sliced
2 tablespoons mixed seeds, for sprinkling

FOR THE HOLLANDAISE SAUCE
2 large egg yolks
100g (3½oz) unsalted butter, cubed
juice of ½ lemon, plus extra to taste
½ teaspoon Dijon mustard
1 teaspoon water
salt

1 Begin by making the hollandaise sauce. Place the egg yolks in a medium-sized glass bowl and half-fill a small saucepan with boiling water. Make sure that the bowl containing the yolks will fit snugly on top of the saucepan without the bowl touching the water, as this will cause the yolks to overheat, but don't place it over the saucepan yet.

2 Melt the cubed butter in a separate small saucepan, then reduce the heat to its lowest setting to keep it warm.

3 Add the lemon juice and mustard to the egg yolks, and season with a pinch of salt. Use a balloon whisk to mix it all together, then place the bowl over the saucepan of water. Set the saucepan over a low heat, and whisk vigorously for 1 minute so the yolks begin to cook and thicken slightly.

4 Drizzle the warm melted butter into the egg yolks 1 tablespoon at a time, whisking well between each addition, until it has all been incorporated. You should be left with a thick, silky-smooth sauce (see my tips overleaf for how to rescue a split sauce!).

5 Add the measured water to loosen the sauce, and season to taste with extra salt and lemon juice. If not using right away, pour the sauce into a small Thermos flask. This will keep it at the correct temperature for pouring for up to two hours without it becoming too thick.

6 To prepare the eggs, bring a medium saucepan of water to a simmer. Crack an egg into a ramekin and slip it into the simmering water; repeat with a second egg. Simmer very gently for 2–3 minutes until the whites are firm, then remove with a slotted spoon and drain on a plate lined with kitchen paper. Repeat with the remaining eggs. You can cook all 4 at once if they will all fit comfortably in your saucepan.

continued overleaf...

MY HOLLANDAISE HAS SPLIT!

Hollandaise sauce is a carefully balanced emulsion of egg yolk and butter, and it can easily split if it gets too hot or isn't whisked quickly enough. If your sauce has split, don't despair. Here are two options to fix it:

1. Have an ice cube on hand. As soon as you notice the sauce begin to split, remove the bowl from the heat and whisk in the ice cube. This should bring the temperature down and the mixture will re-emulsify.

2. Alternatively, crack a fresh egg yolk into a clean bowl. Remove the split mixture from the heat and gradually and slowly pour it into the bowl with the new yolk, whisking constantly. You'll find any lumps will disappear and you'll regain a beautiful smooth sauce.

7. Place the crab meat in a small bowl and pick through it to make sure no pieces of shell remain. Season, then stir in the lemon zest and juice.

8. Toast the crumpets or muffin halves. Place 2 on each plate, then top each with some avocado slices, a heap of dressed crab, a poached egg and finally a drizzle of the hollandaise. Season with freshly ground black pepper and sprinkle with mixed seeds just before serving.

Luscious, velvety scrambled eggs are easy to achieve when you know how, and require next to no effort: win–win! My recipe is simple – just eggs, butter and a few seasonings. The secret is all in the cooking, and keeping it slow and steady. You can easily scale up the recipe to cook for a crowd too.

Scrambled eggs with smoked salmon and chives

Serves 2–3 ~ Preparation time 5 minutes
Cooking time 5–7 minutes

6 large eggs
25g (1oz) salted butter
½ small bunch of chives, finely chopped
freshly ground black pepper

TO SERVE
English muffins, toasted and buttered
smoked salmon
lemon wedges

1 Beat together the eggs vigorously in a measuring jug until they are smooth and no streaks of egg white remain, then season with a good grinding of black pepper and set aside.

2 Choose a large, nonstick frying pan and heat over the lowest setting possible. Add the butter and allow it to melt undisturbed. As soon as the butter has melted, pour the beaten eggs directly into the pool of butter.

3 Slowly and steadily, use a spatula to move the eggs gently around the pan, pushing from the outside to the centre at the top, sides and bottom of the pan, as if you were working your way around a clockface. The eggs should start to ripple, and the uncooked mixture will move into the gaps created. Repeat the process until the eggs are almost completely set, then remove from the heat (they will continue to cook in the residual heat of the pan, so you don't want to take it too far).

4 Sprinkle with chives and serve with hot buttered English muffins, smoked salmon and a wedge of lemon.

Coffee table

I've read that marmalade, once a breakfast-time staple in Britain, is being shunned in favour of jams and chocolate spread. But marmalade's bittersweet tang is precisely what makes it the ideal basis for these cookies. That flavour of orange running through chocolate-rich dough, plus the extra chewiness the marmalade brings, means I always have a stash of these in my freezer, ready to bake.

Double chocolate marmalade cookies

Makes 12 large cookies ~ Preparation time 15 minutes, plus chilling
Cooking time 12–14 minutes

125g (4½oz) salted butter, at room temperature
100g (3½oz) soft light brown sugar
75g (2¾oz) caster sugar
1 large egg
50g (1¾oz) thin-cut Seville orange marmalade
finely grated zest of 1 orange
200g (7oz) plain flour
50g (1¾oz) cocoa powder
½ teaspoon bicarbonate of soda
½ teaspoon baking powder
100g (3½oz) milk chocolate chips

1. In a large bowl, beat together the butter with both the sugars using a wooden spoon, until well combined and smooth – there's no need for it to be light and fluffy. Crack the egg into the mixture and beat again, then stir in the marmalade and orange zest.

2. Tip the flour, cocoa powder, bicarbonate of soda and baking powder into the bowl and fold using a spatula until a stiff dough forms. Stir through the chocolate chips. Cover and refrigerate the dough for 30 minutes (or it can stay chilled for up to 72 hours).

3. When ready to bake, preheat the oven to 200°C (180°C fan/400°F/gas mark 6). Line 2 large baking trays with baking parchment. Using a dessertspoon, scoop out large balls of dough and roll them into balls with slightly damp hands. Place these on the trays, leaving enough space for each one to spread out. You should get 12 large cookies from this mixture.

4. Bake for 12–14 minutes, or until the cookies have spread out and are crispy around the edges. They will look undercooked and puffy in the middle, but this will settle and firm up into a soft, chewy centre. Allow to cool for at least 10 minutes on the tray before enjoying warm. Once cool, these will keep for up to 5 days in an airtight container.

TIP
Once you've rolled the dough into balls, freeze them on a tray lined with baking parchment until solid, then transfer to a freezer-proof container and freeze for up to 6 months. Bake from frozen for 14–16 minutes for fresh cookies on demand.

What makes an excellent last-minute host? A freezer full of ready-to-bake cookies, that's what! Freezing cookie dough has many benefits: it makes sure the butter is cold enough to bake into crisp biscuits, it keeps the shaping even and it allows the flavours to meld together well. These are slightly less chewy than traditional cookies; instead, they have a buttery shortbread-like texture.

Chocolate-chunk freezer cookies

Makes 20 ~ Preparation time 15 minutes, plus chilling
Cooking time 12–15 minutes

220g (7¾oz) salted butter, at room temperature
75g (2¾oz) caster sugar
75g (2¾oz) soft light brown sugar
1 large egg
1 teaspoon vanilla extract
275g (9¾oz) plain flour
75g (2¾oz) white chocolate, chopped into small chunks
75g (2¾oz) dark chocolate, chopped into small chunks

FOR ROLLING
2 tablespoons coarse-grained demerara sugar
1 tablespoon cacao nibs (optional)

1. In a large bowl, beat together the soft butter with both the sugars with an electric whisk or the paddle attachment if using a stand mixer. Beat for 5 minutes until the mixture is light and fluffy. Add the egg and vanilla extract, and beat again until smooth. Tip in the flour and stir using a spatula until a stiff dough forms.

2. Add the white and dark chocolate chunks, and fold into the dough until well distributed.

3. Form the cookie dough into a thick log shape approximately 20cm (8in) long, using a piece of clingfilm or baking parchment to help you. Remove the clingfilm or parchment and roll the log in the demerara sugar and cacao nibs (if using), then rewrap tightly in clingfilm, twisting the ends to seal. Place the cookie dough roll in the freezer and chill until completely frozen. The cookie dough will keep for up to 3 months at this stage.

4. When you are ready to bake your cookies, preheat the oven to 190°C (170°C fan/375°F/gas mark 5) and line a baking tray with baking parchment. Unwrap the log and use a sharp serrated knife to cut 20 slices of frozen dough roughly 1cm (½in) thick. Arrange the cookies, spaced well apart, on the prepared tray.

5. Bake for 12–15 minutes, or until just starting to brown around the edges. The cookies will still feel soft, but will harden as they cool. Allow to cool completely on the tray. These will keep for up to 1 week in an airtight container.

Portable slices of buttery crumble, concealing juicy peach and sticky raspberry jam. You can use other similar stone fruits or berries in this recipe – just make sure nothing is too wet, as the bars won't hold together if there is too much moisture.

Peach and raspberry crumble squares

Makes 20 squares ~ Preparation time 15 minutes
Cooking time 40–45 minutes

175g (6oz) salted butter, chilled
175g (6oz) plain flour
75g (2¾oz) soft light brown sugar
60g (2¼oz) caster sugar
50g (1¾oz) rolled oats
150g (5½oz) raspberry jam
1 ripe peach, stoned and sliced (or 1 × 125g (4½oz) can peach slices in juice (drained) if out of season)
125g (4½oz) raspberries

1. Preheat the oven to 180°C (160°C fan/350°F/gas mark 4). Line a 20cm (8in) square tin with baking parchment.

2. Put the butter and flour into a large bowl and use your fingers to rub together until the mixture resembles breadcrumbs. Add both sugars and rub again until combined, then stir through the oats. If you squeeze the mixture, it should hold together.

3. Tip half the mixture into the bottom of the prepared tin, pushing it right into the corners to form a flat, even layer. Spread the raspberry jam over the top, then top with the peach slices and fresh raspberries. Sprinkle over the remaining crumble topping and bake for 40–45 minutes, or until the topping is golden brown and the jam is bubbling through.

4. Leave to cool to room temperature before slicing into squares. Enjoy cold or warmed up. These bars will keep for up to 4 days in an airtight container.

No one can resist a slice of lemon drizzle loaf, so I've turned a family favourite into a layer cake worth of a cake stand! The fresh mascarpone filling and crisp, lemony top are completely addictive: I challenge you to stop at one slice ...

Lemon drizzle layer cake

Serves 10 ~ Preparation time 30 minutes, plus cooling
Cooking time 20–25 minutes

225g (8oz) salted butter, softened, plus extra for greasing
225g (8oz) caster sugar
4 eggs
225g (8oz) self-raising flour
1 teaspoon baking powder
zest of 2 lemons
1 tablespoon whole milk

FOR THE DRIZZLE
100g (3½oz) granulated sugar
zest and juice of 1 lemon

FOR THE FILLING
125g (4½oz) mascarpone
25g (1oz) icing sugar
100ml (3½fl oz) double cream
juice of ½ lemon

1. Preheat the oven to 180°C (160°C fan/350°F/gas mark 4). Grease 2 × 20cm (8in) sandwich cake tins with butter and line with baking parchment.

2. Using a large bowl and an electric whisk or a stand mixer, cream together the butter and sugar until really light and fluffy. Add the eggs, one at a time, whisking after each addition.

3. In a small bowl, combine the flour and baking powder. Add these dry ingredients to the egg mixture a few tablespoons at a time, and continue to mix until a smooth batter forms. Add the lemon zest and milk, then mix well.

4. Divide the mixture between the prepared tins and use a spatula to smooth over the top. Bake for 20–25 minutes, or until the cakes are golden and well risen, and a skewer inserted into the centre comes out clean.

5. When the cakes have almost finished baking, make the drizzle by mixing together the granulated sugar and lemon zest and juice in a small bowl. Remove the cakes from the oven and use a spoon to drizzle the mixture all over the top of the best-looking sponge layer – it should sink into the warm sponge, leaving a crispy sugar coating on top. Allow the sponges to cool completely in the tins.

6. To make the filling, beat together the mascarpone and icing sugar in a bowl using an electric whisk until smooth, then pour in the double cream and lemon juice. Whisk until thick and billowy.

7. Use the lemon mascarpone cream to sandwich together the two cooled cakes. Store this cake in the fridge to keep the filling fresh. It will keep for up to 3 days.

Sweet and salty treats are a constant craving of mine; I simply cannot resist them! Popcorn creates the base of these no-bake scotcheroo-inspired squares, and they are topped decadently with dark chocolate for bittersweet balance.

Peanut and pretzel popcorn squares

Makes 20 squares ~ **Preparation time** 20 minutes, plus setting
Cooking time 8–10 minutes

2 teaspoons salted butter, plus extra for greasing
50g (1¾oz) salted popcorn
50g (1¾oz) salted pretzels, crushed, plus a handful to top, whole
100g (3½oz) puffed rice cereal
300g (10½oz) golden syrup (or runny honey)
100g (3½oz) soft light brown sugar
250g (9oz) smooth peanut butter
300g (10½oz) dark chocolate (60–70 per cent cocoa solids)

1 Grease a 23cm (9in) square cake tin with butter and line with baking parchment.

2 Combine the popcorn and crushed pretzels in a large mixing bowl and use your hands to break up any large pieces of each. Add the puffed rice and mix well.

3 Combine the golden syrup and brown sugar in a medium-sized saucepan over a medium heat, stirring well. Once bubbling, cook for 1 minute, then remove the pan from the heat and stir in the peanut butter.

4 Use a spatula to pour this hot syrup mixture over the dry ingredients, and quickly mix together until the popcorn, pretzels and rice are completely coated. Tip the mixture into the lined tin and press down gently into an even layer.

5 Melt the dark chocolate in a heatproof bowl set over a pan of barely simmering water, or in short bursts in the microwave. Once smooth, add the butter and stir until melted. Pour this mixture over the popcorn base, tilting the tin to create an even layer. Top with the whole pretzels and leave to set at room temperature for at least 2 hours before slicing into 20 squares. These will keep for up to 5 days stored in an airtight container.

TIP
If 20 squares is too many for your household (or you know you won't be able to resist them!) you can easily halve the quantities for this recipe and set it in a 900g (2lb) loaf tin instead.

Think cinnamon bun meets baklava! Use a tin with a fixed base, not a loose bottom, for these buns, or you'll have a sticky syrup explosion in your oven. An ovenproof frying pan or cast-iron casserole dish will work well if you don't have the ideal tin.

Honey syrup buns

Makes 8–9 buns ~ **Preparation time** 30 minutes, plus rising ~ **Cooking time** 30–35 minutes

25g (1oz) salted butter, plus extra for greasing
125ml (4fl oz) whole milk
125ml (4fl oz) water
1 large egg
500g (1lb 2oz) strong white bread flour, plus extra for dusting
25g (1oz) caster sugar
1 teaspoon salt
7g (2 teaspoons) sachet fast-action dried yeast
vegetable oil, for greasing

FOR THE FILLING
110g (3¾oz) soft light brown sugar
150g (5½oz) runny honey
90g (3¼oz) butter, softened
½ teaspoon ground cinnamon
150g (5½oz) mixed nuts (I like a mix of pistachios, walnuts and almonds), roughly chopped

1. Line a 23cm (9in) round or square cake tin – ideally one with a solid base so the syrup is contained – with a layer of baking parchment and grease the sides with butter.

2. Pour the milk into a small saucepan over a low heat and add the butter. Warm through until the butter has melted, then remove from the heat and add the water. Allow to cool to room temperature, then beat in the egg.

3. Combine the flour, sugar, salt and yeast in a large bowl or the bowl of a stand mixer fitted with a dough hook. Gradually add three-quarters of the milk mixture, mixing until a rough dough forms. Add the remaining milk mixture and continue to mix until you have a soft, sticky dough (you might not need to add all the milk).

4. Tip the dough out on to a lightly oiled surface and knead for around 10 minutes. The dough should be smooth and elastic. Alternatively, use the stand mixer to knead the dough on a low speed for 5–6 minutes. Place the kneaded dough in an oiled bowl, cover with a clean tea towel, and leave to rise for 1–2 hours, or until the dough has doubled in size.

5. While the dough is rising, make the filling by beating together the soft brown sugar, honey and butter in a bowl until smooth and spreadable.

6. Once risen, roll out the dough on a floured surface until you have a large rectangle measuring about 30 × 40cm (12 × 16in). Spread about a third of the filling mixture over the top of the dough in a thin layer using a spatula, then sprinkle with the cinnamon and two-thirds of the chopped nuts.

continued overleaf...

7   Heat the remaining filling mixture in a small saucepan over a medium heat, stirring all the time, for 3–4 minutes, until bubbling and syrupy. Pour into the base of the prepared cake tin, spreading it out to reach the edges, then sprinkle with the remaining nuts.

8   Tightly roll up the dough, starting at the longer side. Use a sharp knife or piece of cotton to trim the ends, then cut the log into 8 pieces for a round tin, or 9 pieces for a square tin. Place the rolls in the tin, cut sides up, nestling them into the syrup, then cover and allow to rise for 30 minutes at room temperature.

9   Preheat the oven to 190°C (170°C fan/375°F/gas mark 5). Once the rolls have risen, place the tin on a baking tray (this will catch any syrup that bubbles over!) and bake for 30–35 minutes, until golden brown and bubbling.

10 Allow to cool for a few minutes, then run a palette knife around the edge of the tin to loosen the rolls. Invert a rimmed plate over the top and carefully flip the tin. Scrape any nuts or syrup that remain in the tin over the top, then serve warm! These buns are best eaten the day of making, or you can reheat them individually for 20 seconds in the microwave.

This simple no-bake slice is a favourite festive treat – a delicious easy win that also makes a great gift. But why limit yourself to the winter months? I enjoy this peppermint chocolate slice all year round!

Peppermint chocolate slice

Makes 24 slices ~ Preparation time 25 minutes, plus chilling

FOR THE BASE
400g (14oz) digestive biscuits
175g (6oz) salted butter
50g (1¾oz) cocoa powder
3 tablespoons golden syrup

FOR THE TOPPING
30g (1oz) salted butter
600g (1lb 5oz) icing sugar
1 teaspoon peppermint extract
6 tablespoons boiling water
200g (7oz) dark chocolate (60–70 per cent cocoa solids), broken into chunks
1 teaspoon vegetable oil

1. Line a 23 × 33cm (9 × 13in) baking tin with baking parchment.
2. To make the base, tip the digestive biscuits into a food processor and blitz into a fine powder. Melt the butter in a small saucepan over a low heat, or in a small bowl in the microwave.
3. Combine the biscuit crumbs, cocoa powder, golden syrup and melted butter in a large mixing bowl, then press into the base of the prepared tin. Press firmly to make sure it is compact and will hold together, then chill for 30 minutes.
4. To make the topping, melt the butter in a small saucepan over a low heat, or in a small bowl in the microwave. Pour into a large bowl, and add the icing sugar and peppermint. Stir, then add the boiling water, a little at a time, continuing to stir until a thick paste forms. When you lift the spoon out, the mixture should settle flat in 15 seconds. If it doesn't, add a little more water.
5. Spread the peppermint mixture over the chilled base, then chill for a further 30 minutes until firm.
6. Melt the chocolate with the oil in a heatproof bowl set over a pan of boiling water until smooth, then pour over the set peppermint layer, tilting the tin so it spreads right to the edges. Allow to set before slicing into 24 squares. These slices will keep for 2 weeks stored in an airtight container.

TIP
If you like, you can add a touch of green food colouring to the mint mixture.

This is a great flourless recipe for our gluten-sensitive friends, but I promise you it will be loved by everyone! Nutty tahini and sesame seeds work beautifully with the chocolate, and the pinch of sea salt on top is a must to make the flavours sing.

Flourless fallen chocolate and sesame cake

Serves 10 ~ **Preparation time** 15 minutes
Cooking time 45–50 minutes

100g (3½oz) salted butter, plus extra for greasing
225g (8oz) dark chocolate (60–70 per cent cocoa solids), broken into chunks
75g (2¾oz) tahini
2 tablespoons cocoa powder
4 eggs
170g (6oz) caster sugar
1 tablespoon sesame seeds
pinch of sea salt flakes
whipped cream, to serve (optional)

1. Preheat the oven to 180°C (160°C fan/350°F/gas mark 4) and grease the base and sides of a 20cm (8in) diameter cake tin generously with butter. Line the base with a sheet of baking parchment (if using a springform tin, I like to use a square of parchment and lay it over the base of the tin before clipping the outside ring on – it's much easier to remove the cake this way).

2. Combine the butter and dark chocolate in a large heatproof mixing bowl set over a pan of boiling water. Once melted, remove from the heat and stir in the tahini. Sift in the cocoa powder before mixing well to combine. Set aside to cool for a few minutes.

3. Separate the eggs, placing the whites into a large, clean mixing bowl. Add the yolks to the bowl of melted chocolate, and once all have been added, mix vigorously to combine.

4. Use an electric whisk to whip the egg whites until they form soft peaks, then add the caster sugar, a few spoonfuls at a time, whisking between each addition, until all the sugar has been incorporated and the mixture is glossy.

5. Dollop the whipped egg whites into the chocolate mixture, then use a balloon whisk to gentle fold the mixture together, using a figure-of-eight motion around the bowl. Stop mixing as soon as everything is combined and no streaks of egg white remain.

6. Pour into the prepared tin, sprinkle with sesame seeds and sea salt flakes, then bake for 45–50 minutes. The top will look cracked and should retain a slight wobble when gently shaken, but should not appear liquid.

7. Allow to cool in the tin to room temperature – the centre will sink down and become fudgy – then transfer to a plate and serve with dollops of whipped cream, if liked. This cake will keep for up to 3 days stored in the fridge – bring it back up to room temperature before serving.

Carrot cake is a fan-favourite (mainly, I believe, because everyone loves anything that is a vessel for cream cheese frosting!) and this heavily spiced loaf is moist and moreish. Make sure you store it in the fridge to keep the frosting firm.

Maple pecan carrot cake loaf

Makes 1 loaf cake ~ Preparation time 25 minutes, plus cooling ~ **Cooking time** 50–55 minutes

butter, for greasing
200g (7oz) soft light brown sugar
125ml (4½oz) olive oil
1 teaspoon vanilla bean paste
2 large eggs
200g (7oz) plain flour
1 teaspoon bicarbonate of soda
1 teaspoon baking powder
1½ teaspoons ground cinnamon
1 teaspoon ground ginger
½ teaspoon ground coriander
1 teaspoon fine salt
175g (6oz) freshly grated carrots (peeled weight)
75g (2¾oz) pecan nuts, roughly chopped

FOR THE FROSTING
80g (2¾oz) full-fat cream cheese
40g (1½oz) unsalted butter, at room temperature
110g (3¾oz) icing sugar
2 tablespoons maple syrup
8 pecan halves

1. Preheat the oven to 190°C (170°C fan/375°F/gas mark 5). Grease a 450g (1lb) loaf tin (see tip) with butter and line with baking parchment.

2. In a large bowl, mix together the sugar, oil, vanilla bean paste and eggs until smooth. Slowly add the flour, bicarbonate of soda, baking powder, cinnamon, ginger, coriander and salt, and continue to beat until well combined.

3. Stir in the grated carrots and chopped pecans, ensuring they are evenly dispersed throughout the mixture. Pour into the lined tin and bake for 50–55 minutes or until golden brown and a skewer inserted comes out clean. Allow to cool in the tin for 20 minutes, then transfer to a wire rack to cool completely before icing.

4. To make the frosting, blend the cream cheese and butter together in a bowl using an electric whisk. Add the icing sugar in several goes until it is all combined, then add 1 tablespoon of the maple syrup and beat briefly to mix. Cover the cooled cake with the frosting, then use the back of a spoon or a small palette knife to swirl it, making a few indentations to catch the syrup. Drizzle with the remaining maple syrup, then stud with the pecan nuts. This cake will keep stored in the fridge for up to 3 days.

TIP
If you've only got a 900g (2lb) loaf tin, your cake will be shallower, so be sure to keep an eye on it, as it will bake more rapidly.

A forager's dream! Browned butter and brown sugar come together to give these blondies a deep caramel flavour, studded with tangy apple, fresh blackberries and hazelnut chunks. Perfect with a hot coffee or chai latte, or warm them up and serve with ice cream for pud.

Autumn blackberry blondies

Makes 16 blondies ~ **Preparation time** 25–30 minutes, plus cooling ~ **Cooking time** 35–40 minutes

150g (5½oz) salted butter, plus extra for greasing
2 large eggs
150g (5½oz) soft light brown sugar
100g (3½oz) caster sugar
210g (7½oz) plain flour
½ teaspoon baking powder
75g (2¾oz) white chocolate, chopped into small chunks
1 Granny Smith apple, cored and finely diced
75g (2¾oz) blackberries
25g (1oz) blanched hazelnuts, roughly chopped

1. Preheat the oven to 190°C (170°C fan/375°F/gas mark 5). Grease a 20cm (8in) square tin with butter and line with baking parchment.

2. In a small saucepan or frying pan, melt the butter over a medium heat. Once it has melted, continue to heat gently for a few minutes more until foaming. Keep cooking until the milk solids have caramelized and gone brown, turning the butter a golden colour, then remove from the heat and allow to cool for 5 minutes.

3. In a large mixing bowl, beat together the eggs with both sugars using a balloon whisk. Drizzle the warm brown butter into the mixture and whisk again until smooth. Switch to a spatula and fold in the flour and baking powder, followed by the white chocolate chunks and three-quarters of the diced apple. Spread the mixture into your prepared tin, then scatter over the blackberries and hazelnuts, along with the remaining apple pieces.

4. Bake for 35–40 minutes, or until risen, golden and firm across the top. Leave in the tin to cool completely, preferably overnight (if you can resist!), so they can become fudgy and dense before being sliced. These blondies will keep for up to 4 days in an airtight container.

A generously sized yet simple cake to celebrate your nearest and dearest! Making your own sprinkles means you can customize the cake to suit your colour scheme or favourite colours, making it perfect for a party. Almond extract is my secret ingredient in buttercream to create that classic 'birthday cake' flavour, but if you do use it, make sure your guests are aware it contains nuts.

Celebration sheet cake

Serves 16 ~ Preparation time 20 minutes
Cooking time 30–35 minutes

250g (9oz) salted butter, softened, plus extra for greasing
400g (14oz) caster sugar
4 large eggs
400g (14oz) self-raising flour
100ml (3½fl oz) whole milk
1½ teaspoons vanilla bean paste

FOR THE BUTTERCREAM
150g (5½oz) unsalted butter, at room temperature
500g (1lb 2oz) icing sugar, sifted
3 tablespoons whole milk or double cream
1 teaspoon vanilla bean paste
½ teaspoon almond extract
¼ teaspoon table salt

1. Preheat the oven to 180°C (160°C fan/350°F/gas mark 4). Grease a 23 × 33cm (9 × 13 in) cake tin with butter and line with baking parchment.

2. Place the butter and sugar in a large bowl if using an electric whisk or in the bowl of a stand mixer and beat for 4–5 minutes, until the mixture is really light and fluffy. Add the eggs, flour, milk and vanilla bean paste and beat again for 2–3 minutes, until smooth and aerated.

3. Scrape the cake mixture into the prepared tin and bake for 30–35 minutes until risen and golden brown on top. A skewer inserted into the middle should come out clean. Allow to cool to room temperature in the tin before icing.

4. To make the buttercream, place the butter in a large bowl or the bowl of a stand mixer and whisk on high until really soft (this makes it easier to incorporate the sugar). Add half the sugar and beat slowly until combined, then add half the milk or cream and beat again. Repeat until the sugar and milk or cream are used up, then add the vanilla bean paste, almond extract and salt and beat on high for at least 5 minutes, until really light and fluffy. Be sure to scrape down the sides of the bowl regularly to catch any stubborn unmixed patches.

5. Pipe or use a palette knife to spread the buttercream over the cooled cake, then top with sprinkles (see opposite). The cake will keep for up to 3 days in an airtight container.

HOMEMADE SPRINKLES

Makes 1 jar ~ Preparation time
20 minutes plus setting

1 large egg white
200g (7oz) icing sugar
few drops of liquid food colouring

1. Line a baking tray with baking parchment.

2. Combine the egg white and icing sugar in a mixing bowl if using an electric whisk or the bowl of a stand mixer and beat together for 2–3 minutes, until really thick and smooth. You're looking for a thick but pipeable consistency; add a very small amount of water or a few tablespoons of extra icing sugar if needed to achieve this.

3. Divide the icing between several bowls (depending on how many colours you want to make) and add the food colouring a little at a time to achieve the colours you'd like. Mix well to incorporate.

4. Transfer the coloured icing into piping bags fitted with small, round-ended nozzles (alternatively, snip the end off a disposable piping bag to create a small hole). Pipe long, thin lines or individual dots on the lined tray, then leave to set for at least 8 hours in a cool, dry place. Once the icing feels dry, use a sharp knife to cut the long lines into small sprinkles.

5. Tip into a small jar and seal until ready to use on cakes, biscuits and desserts.

Roasted strawberries are a kitchen secret I simply adore. Introducing these berries to the oven intensifies their flavour and creates a beautiful, vibrant sauce, which is perfect for serving with a simple yet sophisticated cake like my olive oil sponge. You will need a 2.4 litre (10 cup) bundt tin (see tip).

Olive oil cake with roasted strawberries

Makes 1 bundt cake ~ **Preparation time** 15–20 minutes
Cooking time 50 minutes

175ml (6fl oz) olive oil
3 medium eggs
250g (9oz) full-fat Greek yogurt, plus extra to serve
375g (13oz) caster sugar
300g (10½oz) plain flour
1 teaspoon fine salt
3 teaspoons baking powder
zest of 1 lemon
icing sugar, for dusting

FOR THE LINING PASTE
2 tablespoons olive oil
1 tablespoon plain flour

FOR THE ROASTED STRAWBERRIES
450g (1lb) strawberries
2 tablespoons caster sugar
1 tablespoon lemon juice

1. Preheat the oven to 180°C (160°C fan/350°F/gas mark 4). In a small ramekin, mix together the lining paste ingredients until they form a cohesive mixture. It should be runny enough to spread – add a little more oil if it is not. Use a pastry brush to apply the paste to your bundt tin, making sure to get it into every crevice.

2. In a large mixing bowl, beat together the oil, eggs, yogurt and caster sugar until they form a smooth batter. Sift in the flour, salt and baking powder, and mix until just combined (over-beating will result in a tough sponge). Fold through the lemon zest, then pour into the prepared tin.

3. Bake for 50 minutes, or until the cake is golden on top and a skewer inserted into the middle comes out clean. Allow to cool for 10 minutes in the tin, then turn out on to a wire rack to cool completely.

4. While the cake is baking, hull the strawberries, then slice each one in half (cut any particularly large ones into quarters) and place in a medium-sized roasting tin – they should all fit in one even layer without being too snug. Sprinkle with the sugar and lemon juice, then toss well to coat. Put the strawberries in the oven for the final 20 minutes of cake cooking time, stirring once halfway through. They should be soft, bubbling and surrounded by a vibrant strawberry syrup.

5. Transfer the roasted strawberries and syrup into a small bowl. Dust the top of the cake with icing sugar, then serve slices with a dollop of thick Greek yogurt and a generous helping of the roasted strawberries. This cake will keep for up to 4 days stored in an airtight container.

TIP
If you don't have a bundt tin, you can bake this cake in 2 × 20cm (8in) sandwich tins and freeze one for later, or sandwich them with whipped cream or a simple buttercream. If using a cake tin then bake for 20–25 minutes.

Squeeze round the table

Proper paella is a labour of love. My one-pan version is less needy: it is entirely oven baked. Make sure you use a stainless steel or enamelled roasting dish, rather than one made of glass or ceramic, as metal conducts the heat better and will cook the rice accurately. You'll also get a layer of soccarat – that crispy, caramelized bit on the bottom of the pan – which is arguably the most delicious part of this dish.

Chorizo and cod paella traybake

Serves 4 ~ **Preparation time** 15 minutes
Cooking time 1 hour

125g (4½oz) cooking chorizo (approximately ½ chorizo ring), sliced
1 onion, diced
1 red pepper, sliced
1 tablespoon olive oil
400g (14oz) can chopped tomatoes
150ml (5fl oz) dry white wine
350ml (12fl oz) chicken or vegetable stock
pinch of saffron (optional)
2 teaspoons sweet smoked paprika
300g (10½oz) paella rice
100g (3½oz) green beans, sliced into 2cm (¾in) lengths
4 small cod fillets, about 125g (4½oz) each
1 lemon, cut into wedges
small handful of flat-leaf parsley, chopped
sea salt flakes and freshly ground black pepper

1. Preheat the oven to 200°C (180°C fan/400°F/gas mark 6). In a large roasting tin (about 23 × 33cm/9 × 13in), combine the chorizo, onion and red pepper, then drizzle over the olive oil. Toss to combine, then bake for 15 minutes, stirring halfway through.

2. Meanwhile, tip the tomatoes into a large measuring jug, followed by the wine and stock (swill out the tomato can with a little of the stock to get all the juices), then add the saffron (if using) and 1 teaspoon of the paprika.

3. After 15 minutes, remove the roasting tin from the oven and tip in the paella rice. Stir well, then pour in the tomato and stock mixture and stir again. Cover with foil and bake for 25 minutes.

4. Take off the foil and give the rice a good stir, making sure the rice from the centre gets redistributed to the edges (the corners will cook quickest). Stir in the green beans. Arrange the cod fillets on top of the rice, sprinkle with the remaining paprika and some sea salt flakes, then bake, uncovered, for 20 minutes, gently mixing the rice once more during this time (without disturbing the cod), until the rice is tender and the cod is cooked through. Add a little extra water if the rice isn't cooked through at this point.

5. Top the baked rice with wedges of lemon and parsley, then season generously before serving.

TIP
Replace the cod with other firm white fish, chicken or prawns, if you prefer.

Inspired by elotes, the Mexican street food of spicy, charred corn on the cob, this is a great dish to kick off an evening, and it's easy to scale up to feed a crowd. Tajin seasoning can be hard to come by, but I'd recommend seeking it out where you can, as it packs a smoky, sour, spicy punch that is hard to replicate! Try this as a starter for my Shredded Chicken Fajitas (opposite).

Mexican street corn nachos

Serves 4–6 ~ Preparation time 20 minutes
Cooking time 15 minutes

1 tablespoon olive oil
250g (9oz) sweetcorn kernels, frozen or freshly cut from 2–3 cobs
200g (7oz) tortilla chips
25g (1oz) unsalted butter
25g (1oz) plain flour
350ml (12fl oz) whole milk
150g (5½oz) Red Leicester or mature Cheddar cheese, grated
1 teaspoon cayenne pepper
juice of 1 lime
100g (3½oz) feta cheese
1 teaspoon tajin seasoning (optional)
small handful of coriander, leaves picked

TO SERVE (OPTIONAL)
soured cream
chopped avocado
lime wedges

1. Preheat the oven to 220°C (200°C fan/425°F/gas mark 7). Warm the oil in a large frying pan over a medium heat. Add the sweetcorn and cook for 6–7 minutes, or until golden and beginning to brown, stirring often. Once toasted and cooked through, remove from the heat and set aside.

2. Tip the tortilla chips into a large ovenproof dish and bake for 5 minutes until hot.

3. Meanwhile, melt the butter in a small saucepan over a medium heat, then add the flour and stir to form a paste. Cook, stirring, for 3–4 minutes to cook out the flour, then swap to a balloon whisk and start to gradually add the milk. Once all the milk has been incorporated, you should have a thick, smooth sauce. Stir in the cheese, cayenne pepper and half the lime juice.

4. Pour the cheese sauce over the warm nachos, then top with the toasted corn. Crumble over the feta and squeeze over the remaining lime half, then sprinkle with tajin seasoning and coriander leaves.

5. Serve with soured cream, chopped avocado and lime wedges on the side, if liked.

Smoky chicken fajita filling, cooked up in one pot and shredded to keep it tender and moist. Serve with wraps for next-level fajitas, or over rice with all the toppings for burrito bowls. For the full fiesta experience, blitz up a batch of frozen margaritas to enjoy alongside.

Shredded chicken fajitas

Serves 6 ~ Preparation time 15 minutes
Cooking time 30 minutes

1 teaspoon ground cumin
1 teaspoon smoked paprika
1½ teaspoons ground coriander
1 teaspoon chilli powder
1 teaspoon sea salt flakes
4 large chicken breasts
2 tablespoons olive oil
1 green pepper, sliced
1 red pepper, sliced
1 large onion, finely sliced
400g (14oz) can chopped tomatoes
400g (14oz) can black beans, drained
2 limes, halved

TO SERVE
tortilla wraps
sliced avocado
grated cheese
soured cream
chopped coriander

1. In a large bowl, combine the ground cumin, paprika, ground coriander, chilli powder and salt. Once mixed, add the chicken breasts and toss well until completely coated in the spice blend.

2. Heat 1 tablespoon of the olive oil in a deep cast-iron casserole dish or nonstick pan that has a lid over a medium–high heat. Once hot, add the chicken breasts and sear for 4–5 minutes on each side. You're looking to develop a thick crust and for the spices to begin to blacken. Use tongs to remove the chicken from the pan and set aside on a plate.

3. Add the remaining oil to the pan, followed by the sliced peppers and onion. Fry for 3–4 minutes, stirring often, until beginning to soften, then add the chopped tomatoes and drained black beans. Stir well to combine, then nestle the whole chicken breasts into the mixture, reduce the heat to low and cover with the lid.

4. Simmer, lid on, for 15 minutes, to gently cook the chicken through, then remove the lid and simmer for a further 5 minutes. Remove the chicken to a chopping board and shred using two forks, then return the meat to the pan and stir well to combine. Just before serving, squeeze over the juice of half a lime, and slice the remaining lime and a half into wedges.

5. Serve the shredded chicken with wraps, sliced avocado, cheese, soured cream, lime wedges and chopped coriander, if liked. This recipe is also delicious served on top of rice as a burrito bowl.

Rich, creamy, made in one pan – is this the ideal relaxed dinner-party dish? I think so! You can halve this recipe to serve two, or scale it up and use a large roasting dish to feed a crowd in a fuss-free manner. Use canned cherry tomatoes if you can find them: they add beautiful texture and are sweeter than regular canned tomatoes. Delicious served with couscous, short pasta or rice, and a dressed green salad.

Creamy chicken cacciatore

Serves 4 ~ Preparation time 15 minutes
Cooking time 45–50 minutes

4 large chicken thighs, skin on, bone in
olive oil, for drizzling
1 onion, halved and finely sliced
2 garlic cloves, finely chopped
2 tablespoons capers in brine
1 red pepper, finely sliced
25g (1oz) basil, half roughly chopped, half leaves picked
2 × 400g (14oz) cans cherry tomatoes
125g (4½oz) mascarpone
sea salt flakes and freshly ground black pepper

1 Preheat the oven to 200°C (180°C fan/400°F/gas mark 6) and place a large, ovenproof frying pan over a medium heat. Season the chicken thighs and rub the skin with a small amount of olive oil, then place, skin-side down, in the pan. Cook for 5 minutes until the skin has started to brown and become crisp. Use tongs to remove the chicken and set aside on a plate, leaving any excess oil in the pan.

2 Keep the pan over the heat and add the onion, along with a pinch of salt. Sweat for 8–10 minutes, stirring often, until softened. Add the garlic, capers and red pepper, and fry for a further 5 minutes.

3 Add the chopped basil and canned tomatoes. Bring to a simmer, then stir in the mascarpone until the sauce is creamy.

4 Nestle the chicken thighs back into the pan, skin-side up, leaving the skin above the liquid so it becomes crisp. Season well with salt and pepper, then transfer to the oven and bake for 25–30 minutes. The sauce should have reduced and the chicken should be crisp on top and cooked through.

5 Top with the remaining fresh basil and serve with your chosen accompaniments.

TIP
If you want to double this recipe but don't have an ovenproof frying pan large enough, simply decant the sauce elements into a large roasting tin after they have been cooked. Nestle the seared chicken into the tin and bake as above.

My sister and I always used to order chicken and sweetcorn soup from our local Chinese restaurant. I still rely on this dish to perk me up on grey days, but now I make it myself. The aromatic, ginger-rich base combined with the rich savouriness of the chicken and the pops of sweetness from the corn make for a nourishing meal. I've added noodles to give this soup more substance, perfect for a weeknight dinner.

Chicken and sweetcorn noodle soup

Serves 4 ~ Preparation time 5 minutes
Cooking time 20 minutes

- 2 tablespoons vegetable or toasted sesame oil
- 4 garlic cloves, grated or finely chopped
- 5cm (4in) piece of fresh root ginger, peeled and grated or finely chopped
- 1.25 litres (generous 5 cups) chicken stock
- 2 chicken breast fillets, halved lengthways
- 300g (10½oz) sweetcorn kernels, cut from 3 cobs or frozen
- 2 teaspoons cornflour mixed with 1 teaspoon cold water
- 1 tablespoon light soy sauce
- 2 × 65g (2½oz) nests ramen or thin wheat noodles
- 2 large eggs
- 4 spring onions, trimmed and finely chopped

1. Heat the oil in a large saucepan over a low heat. Add the garlic and ginger and gently fry for 2 minutes until softened.
2. Add the chicken stock to the pan and bring to a gentle simmer. Submerge the chicken in the stock and poach for 10 minutes until thoroughly cooked and no pink meat remains. Remove the chicken using tongs and set aside on a plate. Add the sweetcorn to the simmering stock and cook for 5 minutes, then add the cornflour slurry and soy sauce and stir well to combine.
3. Shred the chicken using two forks, then return it to the soup, along with the noodles, and allow to cook for 3–5 minutes, until the noodles are cooked through. Beat the eggs in a small jug, then pour slowly into the soup in a steady stream, stirring as you do so. The egg will cook immediately and thicken the soup.
4. Stir through half the spring onions, then ladle the soup into bowls and garnish with the remaining spring onions. This is best enjoyed immediately.

TIP
If you want to freeze a portion, do so before adding the eggs and noodles, as they do not defrost well. This is a great recipe for using up leftover roast chicken.

My husband says he can tell when I'm getting ready to cook my favourite dishes because of the smell of garlic wafting out of the kitchen. And he's right! I'm a garlic fiend. This is my take on gambas pil pil, the Spanish tapas dish, turned into a main course – juicy prawns, cooked in bubbling chilli and garlic olive oil, poured over a rich tomato orzo pasta. Lemon wedges bring an essential burst of fresh acidity.

Pil pil prawns with orzo

Serves 4 ~ Preparation time 15 minutes
Cooking time 30 minutes

100ml (3½fl oz) olive oil
1 red onion, finely chopped
6 garlic cloves, finely sliced
1–2 red chillies, deseeded and finely chopped
600g (1lb 5oz) cherry tomatoes, halved
200ml (7fl oz) white wine (see tip)
320g (11¼oz) orzo pasta
600ml (20fl oz) vegetable stock
300g (10½oz) raw king prawns, peeled and deveined
2 teaspoons smoked paprika
small bunch of flat-leaf parsley, finely chopped

TO SERVE
lemon wedges
crusty sourdough bread

1. Heat 2 tablespoons of the oil in a large saucepan or cast-iron casserole dish over a medium heat. Add the onion and fry for 4–6 minutes until softened but not browned. Add half the garlic and half the chilli, then cook for a further minute until fragrant.

2. Add the cherry tomatoes and cook for 5 minutes until beginning to collapse. Pour in the wine and simmer for 2–3 minutes, squashing the tomatoes with the back of a wooden spoon so they release all their juices. Add the orzo, followed by the stock, then reduce the heat and cook for 15 minutes, stirring often, until the pasta is tender and has absorbed most of the liquid. Season to taste, then remove from the heat and cover until ready to serve.

3. Meanwhile, heat the remaining oil in a medium-sized frying pan over a medium–high heat until sizzling. Add the remaining garlic and chilli and fry until the garlic begins to turn golden. Tip the prawns into the infused oil and cook for 2–3 minutes, stirring often, until pink and cooked through. Remove from the heat, stir in the paprika and parsley, and season well.

4. Tip the prawns, along with all the flavoured oil, over the top of the orzo, then serve with lemon wedges and bread to mop up all the juices.

TIP
If you don't want to use wine, simply replace it with an equal volume of extra stock.

My favourite thing about serve-yourself bowl food is that you can tailor your portion exactly to your preferences. Not a fan of aubergine? Just go for the potatoes. Obsessed with whipped feta sauce (as you should be – I could eat the whole bowl)? Smother your plate with it. This is a lovely way to serve moussaka in the summer, complete with flatbreads and a fresh green salad.

Moussaka bowls

Serves 6 ~ Preparation time 30 minutes
Cooking time 45 minutes

500g (1lb 2oz) baking potatoes, sliced into 1cm (½in) discs
2–3 large aubergines, sliced into 1cm (½in) discs
2 tablespoons olive oil, plus extra for drizzling
1 red onion, diced
3 garlic cloves, peeled and finely chopped
1 teaspoon ground cumin
1 teaspoon ground cinnamon
1 teaspoon pul biber (or ½ teaspoon dried chilli flakes)
600g (1lb 5oz) lamb mince
small bunch of oregano, leaves picked
small bunch of thyme, leaved picked
200ml (7fl oz) red wine
400g (14oz) can chopped tomatoes
2 tablespoons tomato purée
sea salt flakes and freshly ground black pepper

FOR THE WHIPPED FETA SAUCE
200g (7oz) feta cheese
150g (5½oz) full-fat Greek yogurt
2 tablespoons extra virgin olive oil, plus extra to drizzle

TO SERVE
100g (3½oz) pine nuts
flatbreads
green salad

1 Preheat the oven to 220°C (200°C fan/425°F/gas mark 7). Layer the potato and aubergine discs in a large roasting tin, overlapping them slightly but keeping to one even layer. Drizzle with olive oil and season well before roasting for 45 minutes until crisp and cooked through.

2 Meanwhile, heat the olive oil in a large frying pan over a medium heat. Add the diced onion and fry for 5–10 minutes until softened, then stir in the garlic, cumin, cinnamon and pul biber. Cook for a further 2 minutes, then add the lamb mince, oregano and thyme, reserving a few tablespoons of the oregano to sprinkle at the end.

3 After 5 minutes, once the mince is browned, add the red wine, chopped tomatoes and tomato purée. Season well with salt and pepper. Simmer for 30 minutes, or until reduced and thickened, then remove from the heat and keep covered until needed.

4 To make the whipped feta topping, crumble the feta into a small food processor and add the Greek yogurt. Blitz for a minute or two until smooth, then add the olive oil and pulse together until the mixture is thick. Decant into a bowl and drizzle with a small amount of olive oil.

5 Toast the pine nuts in a small frying pan over a medium heat for 2–3 minutes until golden brown. Serve each person (or let them help themselves to) a heap of potato and aubergine slices, topped with the lamb sauce and whipped feta, and finished with a sprinkle of toasted pine nuts and the reserved oregano. Have a pile of warm flatbreads on hand to mop up the sauce, and a bowl of fresh green salad too!

Some may argue that these doesn't technically qualify as pies, but when you gather at the dinner table, I promise you that any complainers will go quiet! This recipe is designed to feed a crowd with different tastes – make a batch of the chicken filling for the meat eaters, a batch of the butterbean and pumpkin filling (see opposite) for vegetarians, and enough crispy pastry tops for the whole group.

Chicken and mushroom pot pies

Serves 6 ~ Preparation time 20 minutes
Cooking time 35 minutes

2 tablespoons olive oil
600g (1lb 5oz) skinless, boneless chicken thigh fillets, cut into strips
200g (7oz) chestnut mushrooms, sliced
25g (1oz) salted butter
1 large onion, finely chopped
2 garlic cloves, finely chopped
25g (1oz) plain flour
125ml (4fl oz) white wine
250ml (9fl oz) chicken stock
3–4 thyme sprigs, leaves picked
100g (3½oz) crème fraîche

TO SERVE
6 Pastry Tops (recipe opposite)
green vegetables
mashed potato

1. Heat 1 tablespoon of the oil in a large frying pan over a medium–high heat. Add the chicken and cook for 5–6 minutes, or until lightly browned all over. Remove from the pan using a slotted spoon and set aside in a bowl.

2. Add the remaining oil to the pan and increase the heat to high. Add the mushrooms and fry for 4–5 minutes until well browned. Remove from the pan and add to the bowl with the chicken, ready to add to the sauce later.

3. Reduce the heat to low and add the butter to the pan, followed by the onion. Cook for 10 minutes, stirring often, until soft and translucent. Add the garlic and cook for a further minute, then sprinkle in the flour and stir until all the ingredients are coated.

4. Increase the heat to medium and pour the white wine into the pan, stirring until a thick paste forms. Stir in the chicken stock, thyme and a generous pinch of salt and black pepper, then put the cooked chicken and mushrooms back into the pan. Simmer gently for 8–10 minutes until the liquid is reduced, then mix in the crème fraîche and continue to heat for a further 5 minutes until thickened.

5. Season to taste, then spoon into shallow bowls and serve up with pastry rounds, green vegetables and creamy mashed potato.

TIP
If you want to prepare the filling ahead of time, simply cool and chill in a sealed container for up to 2 days. Reheat thoroughly until piping hot before serving.

Butterbean and pumpkin pot pies

Serves 6 ~ Preparation time 15 minutes
Cooking time 40–45 minutes

1 tablespoon vegetable oil
1 large onion, diced
500g (1lb 2oz) pumpkin or butternut squash, peeled and diced into 2cm (¾in) cubes
2 large garlic cloves, thinly sliced
1 teaspoon ground turmeric
1 teaspoon cumin seeds
1 teaspoon dried chilli flakes
1 teaspoon dried oregano
400g (14oz) can chopped tomatoes
400g (14oz) can butter beans, drained and rinsed
6 Pastry Tops, to serve (recipe below; swap the dried thyme for smoked paprika)
sea salt flakes and freshly ground black pepper

1. Heat 1 tablespoon of the oil in a large, lidded saucepan or casserole dish over a medium heat. Add the onion and gently fry for 8–10 minutes until soft and translucent but not browned. Add the diced pumpkin and garlic, then cook for 5–6 minutes until beginning to soften. Sprinkle in the turmeric, cumin seeds, chilli flakes and oregano, along with a generous pinch of salt and good grinding of black pepper, and mix well to combine.

2. Pour in the canned tomatoes, then fill the can with water and add this to the pan. Stir, cover with a lid, reduce the heat to low and cook gently for 20–25 minutes, stirring occasionally.

3. Once the pumpkin is tender and cooked through, remove the lid and add the butterbeans. Simmer for 2–3 minutes, then turn off the heat and allow to stand for 5 minutes before serving to thicken. Spoon into bowls and top with a pastry round.

PASTRY TOPS

Makes 6
Preparation time 5 minutes
Cooking time 25–30 minutes

320g (11¼oz) sheet ready-rolled all-butter puff pastry
1 egg
1 teaspoon dried thyme
sea salt flakes

1. Preheat the oven to 200°C (180°C fan/400°F/gas mark 6) and line a baking tray with baking parchment.

2. Using an 8–10cm (3¼–4in) round cutter, cut out 6 rounds from the pastry, then transfer to the prepared baking tray. (If you don't have a cutter, use a small bowl and a sharp knife to cut the circles).

3. Beat the egg in a small bowl and use a pastry brush to apply a thin coating to the top of each pastry round. Sprinkle with the thyme and a small pinch of sea salt flakes, then bake for 25–30 minutes until crisp. The cooked pastry rounds will keep for up to 3 days in an airtight container – gently warm them through in the oven before serving.

Bowl food is ideal for entertaining, as your guests can serve themselves according to their appetite, preferences and dietary requirements. Here I've given you everything you need to create delicious hummus bowls, served up with a choice of chicken shawarma or za'atar carrots and chickpeas. Serve with a pile of warm flatbreads, fresh green salad and pomegranate seeds or pickled red onions for a pop of colour.

Hummus bowls with toppings

HOMEMADE HUMMUS

Makes enough for 6 large portions
Preparation time 10 minutes

700g (1lb 9oz) jar chickpeas or
 2 × 400g (14oz) cans chickpeas
1 garlic clove, roughly chopped
100g (3½oz) tahini
½ teaspoon sea salt flakes
juice of 1 lemon
extra virgin olive oil, to serve

1. Drain the chickpeas, reserving about 4 tablespoons of the liquid in a small jug to use later. If you are using canned chickpeas, you can remove the skins at this point if you want a super-smooth hummus by tipping the drained chickpeas into a tea towel, rubbing vigorously and picking out the skins. Jarred chickpeas are soft enough for you to skip this step.

2. Tip the chickpeas into a food processor or blender and add the garlic, tahini, salt and lemon juice. Process the ingredients, adding the chickpea liquid 1 tablespoon at a time, until you get a smooth and creamy paste – this will take around 5 minutes. Make sure to use a spatula to scrape down the sides to ensure every spoonful is well mixed.

3. Taste the hummus and adjust the seasoning as needed. You can add more salt, lemon juice or tahini, according to your preference.

4. Transfer the hummus to a serving dish. Create a swirl pattern on top with the back of a spoon. Drizzle with extra virgin olive oil, then fill the centre with one or both of the topping options on the following page. This hummus will keep for up to 3 days in the fridge, without the toppings.

QUICK SPICED CHICKEN SHAWARMA

Serves 4–6 as a topping
Preparation time 5 minutes, plus marinating
Cooking time 15–20 minutes

juice of 1 lemon
2 tablespoons olive oil
2 teaspoons smoked paprika
1 teaspoon ground cumin
1 teaspoon ground coriander
1 teaspoon sea salt flakes
½ teaspoon ground cinnamon
1kg (2lb 4oz) skinless, boneless chicken thigh fillets

1. Combine the lemon juice and olive oil in a large bowl or lidded container. Sprinkle in the spices and stir to combine, then add the chicken thigh fillets. Turn so that the meat is fully coated in the mixture, then cover and leave to marinate in the fridge overnight, or for at least 1 hour.

2. When you're ready to cook, preheat the oven to 220°C (200°C fan/425°F/gas mark 7). Spread the marinated chicken fillets out on a baking tray and roast for 15–20 minutes until nicely browned and cooked through. The juices should run clear and there should be no pink meat. Leave to rest for a further 5 minutes before slicing and serving.

ZA'ATAR-ROASTED CARROTS AND CHICKPEAS

Serves 4–6 as a topping
Preparation time 10 minutes
Cooking time 40 minutes

3 large carrots, sliced into thin batons
2 tablespoons olive oil
½ teaspoon sea salt flakes
1 teaspoon za'atar
250g (9oz) jarred or canned chickpeas (drained weight), drained and rinsed
1 teaspoon sesame seeds
chopped flat-leaf parsley, to garnish

1. Preheat the oven to 220°C (200°C fan/425°F/gas mark 7).

2. Tip the carrot batons into a large roasting tin and drizzle with the olive oil. Sprinkle with the sea salt flakes and za'atar, then toss to make sure everything is well coated.

3. Bake for 20 minutes, then toss the carrots and add the chickpeas to the roasting tin. Toss to coat, then bake for a further 20 minutes, until the carrots are tender and cooked through. Sprinkle with the sesame seeds and a scattering of chopped parsley, then serve.

Many of the recipes in this chapter can be made in one pot or one pan, as simplicity is key when you're cooking for a crowd. That doesn't mean scrimping on flavour, however, and this sticky traybake is testament to this idea. You many need to use two roasting tins if you don't have one large enough to accommodate all the ingredients in one layer.

Hoisin sausage bake

Serves 4 ~ Preparation time 15 minutes
Cooking time 45 minutes

8 pork sausages
2 tablespoons sesame oil
1 large or 2 small sweet potatoes, skin on, diced into 2cm (¾in) cubes
1 red onion, sliced into wedges
3 large portobello mushrooms, cut into 1cm (½in) slices
160g (5¾oz) hoisin sauce
2 teaspoons light soy sauce
5 tablespoons water
1 red chilli, deseeded and finely chopped
2 garlic cloves, finely chopped
125g (4½oz) Tenderstem broccoli
2 teaspoons sesame seeds
freshly ground black pepper
cooked brown basmati rice, to serve (optional)

1. Preheat the oven to 220°C/200°C fan/425°F/gas mark 7. Arrange the sausages in a large metal or enamel roasting tin (around 35 × 40cm/14 × 16in) and drizzle with with 1 tablespoon of the sesame oil. Place in the oven for 10 minutes to begin cooking.

2. After 10 minutes, remove the tin from the oven and add the sweet potato cubes, onion wedges and mushroom slices. Drizzle with the remaining oil and season well with black pepper, then return to the oven for 25 minutes, turning the sausages halfway through to ensure an even colour on both sides.

3. Meanwhile, mix together the hoisin sauce, soy sauce, measured water, chilli and garlic.

4. Remove the tin from the oven and nestle the broccoli among the sausages and sweet potato cubes, then drizzle the sauce over the whole lot. Sprinkle with the sesame seeds, then return to the oven to roast for 10 minutes until the sauce is bubbling and the sausages are cooked through.

5. Allow to stand for 5 minutes before serving alone or with brown basmati rice.

Perhaps the ultimate comfort food. You'll have no trouble drawing a crowd round your place when this mac and cheese is on the table. Make a big panful, then serve with some of my topping suggestions for people to add at the table to suit their preferences. I'll take a sprinkle of them all!

Stovetop macaroni cheese

Serves 4–6 ~ Preparation time 25 minutes
Cooking time 15 minutes

60g (2¼oz) plain flour
60g (2¼oz) salted butter
½ teaspoon smoked paprika
1 teaspoon Dijon mustard
½ teaspoon garlic granules
525ml (18fl oz) whole milk
170ml (6fl oz) can evaporated milk
150g (5½oz) Cheddar cheese, grated
100g (3½oz) Gruyère cheese, grated
375g (13oz) macaroni pasta

TO SERVE
Crispy Onions (recipe opposite)
chopped red chillies
crispy cooked pancetta
Basil Pesto (recipe below)

1. Bring a large pan of water to the boil and add a big pinch of salt. Add the pasta and cook according to packet instructions until al dente, then drain aside.

2. While the pasta is cooking, make the cheese sauce. Melt the butter in a large saucepan or casserole dish. Once it has completely melted, add the flour and stir until a thick paste forms. Cook the mixture for 1 minute, stirring constantly, to cook out the flour. Add the smoked paprika, mustard powder and garlic granules, then stir again.

3. Gradually add the milk, little by little, until the sauce is completely smooth. Once bubbling, stir in the evaporated milk and both grated cheeses. Mix well until the cheese has melted, then combine the pasta and cheese sauce. Stir well, then cover to keep warm until ready to serve alongside your chosen toppings.

BASIL PESTO

Makes 1 small jar
Preparation time 5 minutes
Cooking time 3–4 minutes

45g (1¾oz) pine nuts
75g (2¾oz) fresh basil (large bunch)
40g (1½oz) aged Parmesan cheese, grated
1 garlic clove, roughly chopped
150ml (5fl oz) olive oil
1 tablespoon lemon juice

1. Gently toast the pine nuts in a small frying pan over a low heat for 3–4 minutes until golden and smelling aromatic. Add to a food processor (or use a large pestle and mortar), along with the basil, Parmesan and garlic. Blitz to combine, then add the olive oil and blend until a smooth paste forms. Stir in the lemon juice and transfer into a jar or serving bowl. It will keep for up to 1 week stored in the fridge.

CRISPY ONIONS

Makes enough topping for 6 people
Preparation time 5 minutes
Cooking time 5–8 minutes

1 large red onion, finely sliced
2 teaspoons cornflour
vegetable oil, for frying
pinch of sea salt flakes

1. In a bowl, combine the red onion and the cornflour and toss well to coat.

2. Pour vegetable oil into a medium-sized, deep-sided frying pan or saucepan to a depth of 3cm (1¼in). Heat gently over a medium–low heat until the oil temperature registers 160°C (320°F) on a cooking thermometer, or a piece of onion sizzles when dropped in. Once the oil is hot enough, add the onion slices and fry for 5–8 minutes, stirring often with a slotted spoon, until they turn golden and crisp.

3. Transfer using a slotted spoon to a plate covered with kitchen paper to blot up any excess oil, then tip into a bowl and sprinkle with sea salt flakes. The onions will keep for up to 3 days in an airtight container.

Full of nourishing spices, creamy coconut milk and a little bit of heat, this dish is a real crowd-pleaser. I also batch-cooked and froze this dahl when I was pregnant, ready to reheat in those blurry weeks with a newborn, and oh, was I grateful that I did! The butterbean and cumin parathas are easy to make, but if you don't have the time or the energy, ready-made naan or chapatis work marvellously well too.

Sweet potato dahl with butterbean parathas

Serves 6 ~ Preparation time 30 minutes
Cooking time 40–45 minutes

FOR THE DAHL
375g (13oz) dried red split lentils
2 tablespoons vegetable oil or ghee
2 shallots, finely chopped
thumb-sized piece of fresh root ginger, peeled and finely chopped
4 garlic cloves, finely chopped
½ green chilli, finely chopped (use the other half for the parathas overleaf)
1½ teaspoons ground cumin
1 teaspoon ground turmeric
½ teaspoon ground coriander
1.1 litres (generous 4½ cups) vegetable stock
400ml (14fl oz) full-fat coconut milk
1 teaspoon salt
260g (9½oz) spinach
juice of 1 lime

FOR THE ROASTED SWEET POTATOES
1kg (2lb 4oz) sweet potatoes, chopped into 2cm (¾in) cubes
1 tablespoon vegetable oil
1 teaspoon cumin seeds
sea salt flakes and freshly ground black pepper

1. Preheat the oven to 220°C (200°C fan/425°F/gas mark 7).

2. Begin with the roasted sweet potatoes. Tip the sweet potato cubes on to a baking tray and drizzle with the oil. Season with salt and pepper, then scatter over the cumin seeds and toss to coat. Bake for 35 minutes, turning once halfway, until tender and beginning to caramelize.

3. Meanwhile, make the dahl. Rinse the lentils in a sieve under running water, then set aside to drain. Heat the oil or ghee in a large heavy-based saucepan, then add the shallots, ginger, garlic and green chilli. Fry, stirring regularly, for 5–6 minutes, until the shallots are soft and the mixture smells fragrant.

4. Add the spices to the pan, then stir and cook for a further minute. Add the lentils and stir well. Pour in the stock and coconut milk, and add the salt. Cover with the lid and allow to simmer for 20 minutes, stirring occasionally to make sure the dahl doesn't get stuck to the bottom of the dish. The lentils will absorb the liquid and the mixture will become thick. Remove the lid, add the spinach and simmer for 5 more minutes, uncovered, or until the dahl has reached your desired consistency and the spinach has wilted. Squeeze in the lime juice to taste.

continued overleaf...

FOR THE PARATHAS

- 400g (14oz) can butterbeans, drained
- 200g (7oz) plain flour, plus extra for dusting
- 1 teaspoon salt
- 1 teaspoon ground cumin
- ½ green chilli, finely sliced
- small bunch of coriander, finely chopped
- 75–100ml (2½–3½fl oz) water
- 1 tablespoon vegetable oil
- 2 tablespoons ghee or salted butter

TO SERVE

- cooked basmati rice
- plain natural yogurt

5. Meanwhile, to make the parathas, tip the butterbeans into a mixing bowl and use a fork or a potato masher to mash them to a paste. Add the flour, salt, cumin, chilli and chopped coriander, and mix well to combine. Pour in the water, a little at a time, stirring until a soft dough forms (you may not need all the water).

6. Knead the dough briefly to make it smooth, then roll out into a large rectangle about 5mm (¼in) thick on a lightly floured surface. Using a pastry brush, coat the surface of the dough with the oil. Roll up the dough tightly into a log shape, then use a knife to slice it into 8 rounds. Cover with a clean tea towel.

7. Heat a large frying pan over a medium–high heat. Place a round of dough, swirl side up, on the work surface and use a rolling pin to roll it out into a 14cm (5½in) circle. Add to the hot pan and fry for 1–2 minutes on each side until charred and cooked through. Rub the ghee or butter over the hot paratha, then set aside on a covered plate to keep warm while you cook the rest.

8. Serve the dahl with basmati rice and the parathas, and top with roasted sweet potatoes and yogurt.

This is one of my go-to meals for one, but it is so full of flavour that it deserves to be shared with others! Raw, unpasteurized kimchi is best for this recipe (and for eating in general) – the smoky, spicy tang and depth of flavour are unmatched. Top each bowl with a fried egg and drizzle of chilli oil for a quick yet nourishing dinner.

Kimchi and prawn fried rice

Serves 4 ~ **Preparation time** 15 minutes
Cooking time 10 minutes

300g (10½oz) uncooked basmati rice (or about 900g/2lb cooked rice)
550ml (19fl oz) water
½ teaspoon salt
8–10 spring onions
2 tablespoons vegetable oil
4 garlic cloves, grated or finely chopped
40g (1½oz) fresh root ginger, peeled and grated or finely chopped
200g (7oz) raw king prawns, peeled and deveined
300g (10½oz) mangetout
250g (9oz) kimchi
2 tablespoons light soy sauce
2 teaspoons sesame oil
4 large eggs
½ teaspoon sesame seeds
crispy chilli oil, to serve (optional)

1. If cooking the rice from scratch, give the basmati rice a quick rinse in a sieve before tipping into a small saucepan with a lid. Add the measured water and salt, then bring to the boil. Once boiling, reduce the heat to the lowest setting and cover with the lid. Cook for 10 minutes until the water has been absorbed, then turn off the heat and allow to stand for 5 minutes. Remove the lid, fluff up the rice and let as much moisture evaporate as you can before using.

2. Slice the green parts of the spring onions into rounds, and cut the white parts lengthways into thin strips. Reserve the green rounds for garnish.

3. Heat the vegetable oil in a large wok or deep frying pan over a medium heat. Add the spring onion whites and stir-fry for 2–3 minutes until soft and beginning to colour. Stir in the garlic and ginger, then add the prawns and mangetout. Stir-fry for 2–3 minutes before adding the kimchi and cooking for a further minute. Finally, add the cooked rice, along with the soy sauce, and fry for a further 2–3 minutes until piping hot.

4. Meanwhile, heat the sesame oil in a large nonstick frying pan. Once hot, add the eggs, sprinkle with sesame seeds and fry for 3–4 minutes until the edges are crisp and the whites are completely set.

5. Serve the fried rice in large bowls, each topped with an egg and a drizzle of crispy chilli oil (or more sesame oil, if you prefer). Garnish with the reserved spring onion greens.

Table for two

An ideal throw-together starter – ready in minutes and singing with zingy lime and smoky notes from the paprika and searingly hot pan. These peppers make the perfect accompaniment to any tequila-based cocktail – try them with my Rhubarb Paloma (page 198).

Padron peppers

Serves 2 as a starter ~ **Preparation time** 5 minutes
Cooking time 4–5 minutes

2 tablespoons olive oil
150g (5½oz) Padron peppers, left whole
juice of ½ lime
¼ teaspoon smoked paprika
pinch of sea salt flakes

1. Heat the olive oil in a large frying pan over a high heat for 1–2 minutes. Make sure the peppers are completely dry, then add them to the pan and cook for 4–5 minutes, turning often, until they are blistered all over and beginning to wilt.

2. Squeeze the lime juice over the peppers, toss to coat, then sprinkle with the paprika and a generous pinch of sea salt flakes. Tip into a serving bowl and serve immediately, preferably alongside a chilled glass of Spanish wine or a cocktail.

This easy starter gives a whole new meaning to 'date night'! Molten cheese, sticky dates coated in crispy bacon or pancetta lardons, maple syrup and toasted pecans – grab the bread and dive in.

Baked camembert with sticky dates

Serves 2 ~ Preparation time 5 minutes
Cooking time 15–20 minutes

1 camembert wheel (about 250g/9oz)
75g (2¾oz) diced bacon or pancetta lardons
25g (1oz) pecan nuts, roughly chopped
3 pitted Medjool dates, roughly chopped
1 tablespoon maple syrup
1 rosemary sprig, leaves picked
crusty bread, to serve

1. Preheat the oven to 200°C (180°C fan/400°F/gas mark 6). Unwrap the camembert and place in a small round baking dish that is fractionally larger than the cheese, or use its box (lined with a piece of baking parchment) if the cheese came in a wooden container. Score a circle on the top around 1cm (½in) from the edge.

2. Bake the camembert for 15–20 minutes until the top is turning golden and feels squidgy when gently pressed.

3. Meanwhile, fry the bacon or pancetta in a small frying pan over a medium heat for 4–5 minutes until crisp. Add the pecans and dates, and cook for a further 2–3 minutes until the skin of the dates begins to blister. Remove from the heat and stir in the maple syrup and rosemary leaves.

4. Use a sharp knife to prise open the camembert and remove the top circle of rind that you scored earlier. Discard. Fill the centre with the sticky date mixture, then return to the oven for 2–3 minutes to let everything melt together. Serve piping hot with hunks of fresh bread for dipping.

This simple salad makes a great light supper, or a starter for a fancier occasion. To enjoy this at its best, serve the halloumi as soon as it comes out of the oven so it doesn't become rubbery.

Hasselback halloumi and orange salad

Serves 2 ~ **Preparation time** 5 minutes
Cooking time 25–30 minutes

75g (2¾oz) quinoa
2 tablespoons olive oil
2 blush oranges
250g (9oz) block of halloumi
2 tablespoons runny honey
½ red chilli, finely sliced
90g (3¼oz) lamb's lettuce or watercress
sea salt flakes and freshly ground black pepper

1. Place the quinoa in a saucepan with 225ml (8fl oz) water. Bring to the boil, then simmer for 15–20 minutes until the quinoa is cooked and the water has been absorbed. Remove from the heat and stir through 1 tablespoon of the olive oil. Season and set aside to cool.

2. Cut away the skin and pith of the oranges, then slice into wedges, keeping any juices.

3. Use a sharp knife to diagonally score the top of the halloumi, leaving 1cm (½in) between each cut and slicing halfway down the block. Place in a small roasting dish, then rub with the remaining olive oil. Preheat the grill to high and, once hot, grill the halloumi for 6–7 minutes until golden brown and blistered. Drizzle with the honey and scatter over the chilli, before grilling for a further 30 seconds to become bubbly.

4. In a large bowl, toss the quinoa with the lamb's lettuce and any juices from slicing the oranges. Divide between 2 bowls, then top with the orange wedges.

5. Serve the roasted halloumi piping hot in the centre of the table, ready to scoop some on to each plate.

Sea bream is a dense, full-flavoured white fish that stands up well against the punchy Chinese-style salt-and-pepper seasoning. If you can't find it, sea bass is a great alternative. Here, I've served it with rice, but it's also delicious with noodles. A healthy, homemade takeaway treat in the comfort of your own home.

Salt-and-pepper sea bream

Serves 2 ~ Preparation time 15 minutes
Cooking time 8–10 minutes

2 sea bream (or sea bass) fillets, about 90g (3¼oz) each
1 tablespoon vegetable oil
1 fat garlic clove, sliced into thin matchsticks
2.5cm (1 in) piece fresh root ginger, peeled and sliced into thin matchsticks
2 pak choi, halved lengthways
1 small red chilli, finely chopped
2 spring onions, finely chopped
1 tablespoon light soy sauce
juice of ½ lime
cooked jasmine rice, to serve

FOR THE SEASONING BLEND
1 teaspoon sea salt flakes
1 teaspoon soft light brown sugar
½ teaspoon Chinese five-spice
¼ teaspoon crushed chilli flakes
¼ teaspoon ground ginger
¼ teaspoon ground white pepper

1. Combine the seasoning ingredients in a small bowl, breaking up any large chunks of sugar.

2. Pat dry the sea bream fillets, then place on a plate and season generously on both sides with the seasoning mixture, rubbing it into the flesh. Allow to absorb for 5 minutes.

3. Heat the vegetable oil in a large frying pan over a medium heat. Once hot, add the garlic and ginger and stir-fry for 1 minute before pushing to one side of the pan. Place the fish fillets and pak choi in the pan, skin-side down, and cook for 4–5 minutes, until the skin of the fish is crisp and the flesh is almost cooked through. Carefully turn the fish and the pak choi over and cook for a further minute on the other side before removing from the pan and setting aside on a plate.

4. Add the chopped chilli and spring onion to the pan, along with the soy sauce and lime juice. It will bubble up as you add it – use a spatula to stir it vigorously around the pan to release any flavour.

5. Serve the fish and pak choi on a bed of rice, then pour over the juices and aromatics from the pan.

Don't be put off by the lengthy ingredients list here as each item serves a purpose and results in the most incredibly delicious sauce, reminiscent of the one served at the famous l'Entrecôte in Paris. Their sauce is a closely guarded secret, but I've tried my best to replicate it. This is ideal for a date night or when you're treating someone special.

Café de Paris steak and chips

Serves 2 ~ **Preparation time** 45 minutes
Cooking time 30 minutes

2 large floury potatoes, sliced into chips 5mm (¼in) thick
olive oil
2 high-quality sirloin steaks, around 2cm (¾in) thick and 230g (8oz) each
1 garlic clove
25g (1oz) salted butter
green salad, to serve
sea salt and freshly ground black pepper

FOR THE SAUCE
125g (4½oz) unsalted butter
1 shallot, sliced
1 tablespoon finely chopped tarragon
2 tablespoons finely chopped flat-leaf parsley
2 basil leaves
5 anchovy fillets in oil
1 teaspoon capers, in brine, from a jar
3 walnut halves, roughly chopped
¼ teaspoon grated nutmeg
1 small egg yolk
juice of ½ lemon
½ teaspoon Dijon mustard

1. Remove the steaks from the fridge an hour before cooking to take off the chill, and open any packaging to dry them out. Preheat the oven to 220°C (200°C fan/425°F/gas mark 7).

2. Arrange the chips on a baking tray, drizzle with 1 tablespoon of the olive oil and season with salt and pepper before tossing well to coat. Bake for 30 minutes, turning halfway through, until golden and crisp.

3. To make the sauce, melt 25g (1oz) of the unsalted butter in a small saucepan over a medium heat. Add the shallots and cook for 3–4 minutes until they are soft and translucent, but not coloured. Reduce the heat to low and add the remaining 100g (3½oz) butter. Once melted, add the chopped tarragon and parsley, basil, anchovies, capers, walnuts and grated nutmeg. Stir to combine, then aside to cool slightly. Use a stick blender or transfer the mixture into a food processor to blitz until smooth.

4. Using 1 teaspoon olive oil, oil the steaks and season well with salt and pepper. Heat a large frying pan over a high heat until searing hot, then add the steaks to the pan. Try not to move them; you want them to develop a thick, flavoursome crust on the base. After 3–4 minutes, turn the steaks over. Add the garlic clove and butter to the pan at this point, and gently swirl so the butter surrounds the steaks as it melts. Cook for a further 2–3 minutes (longer if you're after more well-done steaks), basting the meat in the butter, then transfer to a chopping board and cover loosely with foil to rest for 5–10 minutes.

continued overleaf...

5 While the steak is resting, finish off the sauce by whisking the egg yolk with the lemon and Dijon mustard in a jug. Once smooth, add the melted butter mixture 1 tablespoon at a time, whisking well after each addition. You should end up with a thick, creamy, emulsified sauce. Pour the sauce into the small saucepan that was used earlier and heat very gently for a few minutes. Taste and season to your liking.

6 Slice the steak and transfer to 2 warm plates. Cover with the sauce, then pile on the chips. Serve with peppery green salad – watercress or rocket are ideal.

The wiggly ribbons of malfadine pasta grip on to the buttery sauce so well and look so pretty with their fluted edges. I use preserved lemon to add complexity to the acidic fresh lemon, but it isn't essential if you can't get hold of them. And if you can't find malfadine pasta, you can use tagliatelle instead.

Courgette and golden garlic malfadine

Serves 2 ~ Preparation time 5 minutes
Cooking time 15 minutes

180g (6oz) malfadine or malfada corta pasta
2 tablespoons olive oil
3 garlic cloves
1 courgette, halved lengthways and sliced into half-moons
1 mint sprig, leaves picked and finely chopped
small handful of flat-leaf parsley, finely chopped
zest and juice of ½ lemon
2 preserved lemons, deseeded and finely sliced
45g (1¾oz) salted butter
25g (1oz) aged Parmesan cheese, finely grated
sea salt and freshly ground black pepper

1. Bring a large saucepan of salted water to the boil, cook the pasta according to the packet instructions, then drain, reserving about 200ml (7fl oz) of the cooking water.

2. Meanwhile, heat the olive oil in a medium frying pan over a medium heat. Slice 2 of the garlic cloves lengthways, as finely as possible. Add to the hot oil and fry for around 30 seconds–1 minute, stirring constantly. As soon as you see a hint of gold, remove the garlic from the pan using a slotted spoon and place on a plate lined with kitchen paper. Leave the remaining oil in the frying pan.

3. Add the courgette to the garlic-infused oil; try to spread the slices in an even layer over the base of the pan so they cook at the same rate. Leave to fry, undisturbed, for 3–4 minutes, until the undersides turn golden, then flip and brown on the other side. Do this in batches if necessary. Add the herbs, lemon zest and preserved lemons to the pan and cook for 1 minute more.

4. Add the butter to the pan and finely grate in the remaining garlic clove. Season with black pepper. Cook for a few minutes, then stir in the lemon juice and a slosh of pasta water (about 150ml/5fl oz, or enough to make a creamy sauce).

5. Add the drained pasta to the sauce and toss well to coat, adding some extra pasta water to loosen if needed. Divide between 2 shallow bowls, and top each with a generous grating of Parmesan, some freshly ground black pepper and the golden garlic pieces. Serve immediately.

A meat-free meal that is spicy, rich and satisfying! Intensely flavoured gochujang and peanut butter add body to the sauce, and the pulled crispy mushrooms will soon become your new addiction.

Pulled crispy mushroom udon noodles

Serves 2 ~ Preparation time 10 minutes
Cooking time 25 minutes

175g (6oz) king oyster mushrooms (or oyster mushrooms)
½ tablespoon sesame oil
1 tablespoon vegetable oil
1 tablespoon tamari soy sauce (or regular dark soy sauce)
125g (4½oz) green beans, trimmed and sliced into batons
300g (10½oz) quick-cook or fresh thick udon noodles

FOR THE SAUCE
4 tablespoons tamari soy sauce (or regular dark soy sauce)
1 teaspoon gochujang paste
50g (1¾oz) smooth peanut butter
2 garlic cloves, finely grated
3cm (1¼in) piece of fresh root ginger, peeled and finely grated
1 tablespoon soft light brown sugar
juice of ½ lime
100ml (3½fl oz) water

TO GARNISH
2 spring onions, finely chopped
2 tablespoons roasted peanuts, roughly chopped
lime wedges, to serve

1. Preheat the oven to 220°C (200°C fan/425°F/gas mark 7). Shred the oyster mushrooms using two forks, then place in a small roasting tin. Toss with the sesame oil, vegetable oil and tamari, then roast for 20 minutes or until crispy and caramelized.

2. Meanwhile, add the sauce ingredients to a deep frying pan over a medium heat and whisk to combine. Bring to a simmer and leave to cook for 3–4 minutes.

3. At the same time, bring a saucepan of water to the boil. Add the green beans and udon noodles, and boil for 3 minutes until the noodles are cooked through and the beans are al dente. Drain, then add the noodles and green beans to the pan of sauce and toss well to combine, adding a little more water if needed.

4. Divide between 2 bowls, then top with the crispy mushrooms. Finish with the chopped spring onions, a sprinkle of peanuts and a squeeze of lime just before serving.

A hot take (quite literally) on a classic: creamy carbonara. I've kept this true to the original and not added any cream, with all the richness coming from egg yolk and starchy pasta water. Add a touch more 'nduja if you're a big spice-lover!

'Nduja carbonara

Serves 2 ~ Preparation time 5 minutes
Cooking time 15 minutes

175g (6oz) dried spaghetti
60g (2¼oz) diced guanciale (or pancetta)
2 garlic cloves, peeled and crushed with the flat of a knife
20g (¾oz) fresh 'nduja (see tip)
4 large egg yolks
45g (1¾oz) Parmigiano Reggiano cheese, finely grated, plus extra to serve
freshly ground black pepper
chopped chives, to serve

1. Bring a large saucepan of salted water to the boil, add the spaghetti and cook for 9–11 minutes or until al dente.

2. While the pasta is cooking, place a deep frying pan over a medium heat. Add the guanciale and, once the fat begins to sizzle, add the flattened whole garlic cloves to the pan. Stir occasionally and cook for 4–5 minutes, until the guanciale is crisp and cooked through. Add the 'nduja and cook for 1–2 minutes more, then remove the garlic from the pan, discard it and turn off the heat.

3. In a small bowl or jug, beat together two of the egg yolks with the Parmigiano Reggiano and a generous grinding of black pepper. Add 2 tablespoons of the pasta water and mix to make a paste.

4. Once the spaghetti is cooked, use tongs to transfer the pasta from the cooking water to the guanciale and 'nduja pan. Toss to combine, making sure the pasta is completely coated. By now, the pan should have cooled slightly, so you can add the sauce without the risk of scrambling the eggs. Pour the sauce directly on top of the pasta, together with a ladleful of the pasta water, then vigorously toss using the tongs. Continue to agitate the pan, adding more cooking water as needed, until the sauce is creamy, heated through and coats every piece of pasta. If the sauce doesn't become thick and creamy, return the pan to a very low heat and toss the pasta constantly until it does.

5. Divide between 2 bowls, and top each one with an egg yolk, a generous amount of freshly grated Parmigiano Reggiano and a sprinkle of chives. Burst the egg yolk and stir it through the pasta just before eating to boost the richness of the sauce.

TIP
The jarred vers of 'nduja will work if you can't get fresh, but it is often less spicy, so add an extra 10g (¼oz).

Whenever I travel, I get a large amount of joy from sampling all the regional specialities I can find. Austrian wiener schnitzel is one such joy, especially when served with salty french fries and sweet lingonberry or cranberry sauce. It is traditionally made with veal cutlets, but these can be difficult to source ethically, so I opt for pork loin instead.

Crispy pork schnitzel with lingonberry sauce

Serves 2 ~ Preparation time 20 minutes
Cooking time 20–25 minutes

2 × 150g (5½oz) boneless pork loin steaks or leg escalopes, fat trimmed
25g (1oz) plain flour
100g (3½oz) panko breadcrumbs
1 egg
5 tablespoons vegetable oil
50g (1¾oz) salted butter
4–6 sage leaves
sea salt and freshly ground black pepper

FOR THE SAUCE
100g (3½oz) lingonberries or cranberries, fresh or frozen
75g (2¾oz) caster sugar
1 tablespoon water

TO SERVE
peppery green salad leaves, such as watercress or rocket
lemon wedges

1. Begin by making the sauce. Combine the berries, sugar and measured water in a small saucepan over a low heat and bring to a gentle simmer. Stir until the sugar has dissolved, then allow the mixture to bubble for 5–10 minutes (depending on whether you've opted for fresh or frozen berries) until thickened and tender. Allow to cool to room temperature, or spoon into a sterilized jar to use later.

2. Season the pork well on both sides and bash any thick parts of the meat with a rolling pin or meat mallet so they are of equal thickness and approximately 1cm (½in).

3. Tip the flour on to a plate and the breadcrumbs on to another, and beat the egg in a shallow bowl. Take the first piece of pork and coat it first in flour, then in the egg and finally the breadcrumbs, making sure the meat is completely coated. Place on a baking tray and repeat with the remaining piece of pork.

4. Pour the oil into a large frying pan over a medium heat and add the butter. When bubbling, add the schnitzels to the pan and fry gently for 3 minutes on each side, until golden brown and cooked through. Blot up any excess oil on the schnitzels and set aside. Finally, fry the sage leaves in the remaining oil until crisp.

5. Serve the schnitzels hot, topped with crispy sage and a generous helping of lingonberry sauce, with a mound of peppery salad on the side and a wedge of lemon to squeeze over the top.

TIP
To sterilize your jar, wash thoroughly with hot soapy water, rinse, then place (including the lid) in a preheated oven at 120°C (100°C fan/250°F/gas mark ½) for 15 minutes. Allow to cool slightly before using.

Kashmiri chilli powder is the secret ingredient in the marinade for these flavoursome salmon skewers. It's bright red, fragrant and fruity, with a mild heat rather than an intense spice. If you're using a different chilli powder, make sure you reduce the quantity. These are also excellent cooked on the barbecue.

Salmon tikka skewers with mango kachumber salad

Serves 2 ~ Preparation time 20 minutes, plus marinating
Cooking time 10 minutes

2 skinless salmon fillets (260g/9½oz total weight), cut into chunky cubes
½ lemon, cut into wedges
½ red onion, cut into wedges
naans, to serve

FOR THE MARINADE
2 garlic cloves, grated
2.5cm (1in) piece of fresh root ginger, peeled and grated
1 teaspoon garam masala
½ teaspoon Kashmiri chilli powder
½ teaspoon ground cumin
½ teaspoon ground turmeric
1 tablespoon lemon juice
3 tablespoons natural yogurt, plus extra to serve
1 teaspoon salt

FOR THE MANGO KACHUMBER SALAD
1 large tomato, deseeded and finely diced
¼ cucumber, deseeded and finely diced
½ red onion, finely chopped
½ small mango (about 75g/2¾oz), peeled and cubed
juice of ½ lemon
pinch of sea salt
10g (¼oz) coriander, finely chopped

1. In a shallow bowl, mix together the marinade ingredients. Add the salmon cubes, then cover and chill for at least 30 minutes, or you can marinate the salmon in advance for up to 2 days.

2. To make the salad, combine the tomato, cucumber, red onion and mango in a salad bowl. Squeeze in the lemon juice, season with salt and add the coriander. Toss well to combine, then set aside.

3. Preheat the grill to high and line a baking tray with baking parchment. Thread the salmon cubes on to the skewers, alternating pieces of salmon with lemon wedges and red onion wedges. Place on the baking tray and grill for 10 minutes, turning the skewers halfway through. The salmon should be cooked through and develop a gentle char.

4. Serve the skewers immediately with warm naans, dollops of natural yogurt and the kachumber salad.

TIP
You will need 2 long skewers or 4 shorter ones – ideally metal ones. If using wooden skewers, soak them in warm water for 10–30 minutes before grilling.

Cacio e pepe *translates as 'cheese and pepper', a deceptively simple-sounding name for the amalgamation of two glorious ingredients. Use tangy sheep's-milk Pecorino and the freshest black pepper you can get your hands on. Gnocchi isn't traditional here (neither is lemon juice!), but it is perfect for the sauce, and the high starch content helps the notoriously unstable emulsion remain creamy and smooth.*

Cacio e pepe gnocchi

Serves 2 ~ **Preparation time** 5 minutes
Cooking time 10–15 minutes

2 teaspoons freshly ground black pepper (see tip), plus extra to serve
50g (1¾oz) unsalted butter
1 tablespoon lemon juice
60g (2¼oz) Pecorino cheese, finely grated, plus extra to serve
450g (1lb 2oz) fresh gnocchi
sea salt

1. Bring a large saucepan of salted water to the boil. (Don't go overboard with the salt here, or the resulting dish will be too salty. The water should have a gentle salinity, but not taste like the sea.)

2. Add the black pepper to a deep frying pan over a low heat. Toast for 2–3 minutes until fragrant, then add the butter and allow to melt completely. Stir in the lemon juice and shake the pan to emulsify, then add the grated Pecorino, stir briefly, and turn off the heat. Allow the cheese to melt in the pan's residual heat.

3. Drop the gnocchi into the boiling water and cook according to the packet instructions (usually around 3 minutes). Once the gnocchi floats and is cooked through, but not mushy, drain over a jug, saving the starchy water from the pan.

4. Add 5 tablespoons of the gnocchi water to the sauce and return the pan to a low heat. Shake and stir vigorously to emulsify; it should appear creamy and smooth.

5. Add the cooked gnocchi to the sauce, tossing well until completely coated, adding an extra splash of the cooking water to loosen the sauce if needed. Heat gently until thickened slightly, then divide between 2 bowls and serve immediately with more freshly ground pepper and extra Pecorino, to sprinkle.

TIP
Grind the black pepper into a ramekin or small bowl until you have enough to measure out 2 teaspoons.

Picnic table

This salad is perfect with a charcuterie board, as part of a summer spread, or just something to take down to the beach in your favourite picnic container. Refreshing, sweet and delicious!

Melon, chilli and mozzarella salad

Serves 4 ~ Preparation time 10 minutes

1 cantaloupe melon, halved and deseeded
220g (7¾oz) cherry tomatoes, halved
small handful of mint, leaves picked and finely chopped
1 large red chilli, finely chopped (discard the seeds and membranes if you prefer a milder flavour)
3 tablespoons extra virgin olive oil
1 teaspoon white wine vinegar
pinch of salt
125g (4½oz) mini mozzarella balls (or 1 large mozzarella ball, torn into pieces)

1. Chop the melon into small chunks, or use a melon baller or teaspoon measure to create curls or balls of melon. Place in a large bowl with the tomatoes.

2. In a small bowl, combine the mint and chilli with the olive oil, white wine vinegar and a pinch of salt. Mix well, then drizzle this mixture over the melon and tomatoes and toss to coat.

3. Add the mozzarella and serve straight away, or cover and store for up to 2 days, keeping the mozzarella separate until you're ready to eat.

The food of the Middle East is captivating: bold, earthy spices combined with bursts of citrus and pops of sweetness. We had Lebanese mezze as our wedding feast when we got married, with this roasted red pepper dip as a centrepiece. Every time I blitz up a bowl of this dip, I'm transported back to that day and reminded of how easy it is to make. Pack into a container with a pile of flatbreads to take on a picnic.

Red pepper muhammara dip

Serves 4 ~ Preparation time 20 minutes
Cooking time 20–25 minutes

3 red peppers
75g (2¾oz) walnuts, chopped
1 garlic clove, chopped
1 teaspoon pul biber (or ½ teaspoon dried chilli flakes)
25g (1oz) soft fresh breadcrumbs (about 1 slice of bread)
2 tablespoons olive oil, plus extra to serve
2 tablespoons pomegranate molasses
juice of ½ lemon
sea salt and freshly ground black pepper
flatbreads, to serve

1 Preheat the oven to 240°C (220°C fan/475°F/gas mark 9) and place the peppers on a baking tray. Roast for 20–25 minutes, turning halfway, until the skin is blackened and crispy. Alternatively, you could use the grill. Place in a bowl and cover with a plate for a few minutes to steam (this will make the skins easier to remove). When cool enough to handle, remove the skin and seeds, and roughly chop the flesh.

2 Tip almost all the walnuts into a food processor, and add the garlic, pul biber and breadcrumbs. Pulse a few times until well combined. Add the red peppers, olive oil, pomegranate molasses and lemon juice, and blitz again until well combined and resembling hummus – if needed, add a little more oil until it looks smooth and creamy.

3 Season with salt, pepper and more pul biber, to taste. Top with drizzle of olive oil and the remaining walnuts just before serving with flatbreads.

Sausage rolls are the food that disappears quickest in our house, thanks to my pastry-fiend husband. I expect he will pass on his love for them to our son, so I'd better get the freezer stocked pronto! These sausage rolls are inspired by pork larb, the national dish of Laos that combines pork mince with fresh herbs, hot chillies and zingy lime. A flavour sensation!

Pork larb sausage rolls

Makes 10 rolls ~ Preparation time 25 minutes
Cooking time 30–35 minutes

1 tablespoon vegetable oil
1 red onion, finely diced
2 lemongrass stalks, finely chopped
1 red chilli, finely chopped (seeds and membranes removed if you want a milder flavour)
2 garlic cloves, finely chopped
400g (14oz) pork sausage meat
juice of 1 lime
1 tablespoon fish sauce
small handful of coriander, finely chopped
320g (11¼oz) sheet ready-rolled all-butter puff pastry
plain flour, for dusting
1 egg, beaten
½ teaspoon dried chilli flakes

1. Preheat the oven to 200°C (180°C fan/400°F/gas mark 6) and line a baking tray with baking parchment.

2. Heat the oil in a frying pan over a medium heat. Add the diced red onion and lemongrass, then fry for 5 minutes until beginning to soften. Add the chilli and garlic, and cook, stirring often, for a further 2–3 minutes. Remove from the heat, tip into a large bowl and allow to cool to room temperature.

3. Once cool, add the sausage meat to the bowl, along with the lime juice, fish sauce and coriander. Mash everything together using a fork or squeeze together using your hands until you have a consistent mixture.

4. Unroll the pastry into a rectangle measuring about 23 × 35cm (9 × 14in), and halve lengthways to create two long rectangles.

5. Divide the sausage meat mixture in half and roll on a floured surface into two long, thin sausage shapes. Make sure they are of an even thickness so the sausage rolls are all the same size.

6. Place one of the long sausage shapes on the first pastry strip. Brush the edges of the pastry with a little beaten egg, then roll up the sausage roll tightly. Repeat with the second pastry strip and sausage shape, then slice each sausage roll into 5 smaller pieces.

7. Place the rolls, seam-side down, on the prepared baking tray, then brush the tops of the sausage rolls with the remaining beaten egg. Make several diagonal cuts on the top of the pastry and sprinkle with chilli flakes. Bake for 30–35 minutes, or until golden brown and cooked through.

8. Eat warm, or cool completely and enjoy as an on-the-go snack. These will keep for up to 3 days stored in an airtight container in the fridge.

Peppery leaves really complement the rich cheesy dough in these scones: here I've used rocket but watercress is equally delicious. Overkneading and overhandling the dough results in tough scones that don't fully rise in the oven, so for best results keep each step as brief as possible.

Cheese and rocket scones

Makes 8 scones ~ Preparation time 15 minutes
Cooking time 20–25 minutes

300g (10½oz) self-raising flour, plus extra for dusting
75g (2¾oz) salted butter, chilled and cubed, plus extra to serve
130g (4¾oz) mature Cheddar cheese, grated
50g (1¾oz) aged Parmesan cheese, grated
50g (1¾oz) wild rocket, finely chopped, plus whole leaves to garnish
135ml (4½fl oz) whole milk
1 egg, beaten
freshly ground black pepper

1. Preheat the oven to 200°C (180°C fan/400°F/gas mark 6) and line a baking tray with baking parchment.

2. Tip the flour into a large bowl and add the cubes of butter. Rub the butter into the flour using your fingertips until the mixture resembles fine breadcrumbs. Stir in the grated cheeses and chopped rocket, season well with black pepper and make a well in the centre.

3. Gradually pour the milk into the centre of the well, stirring with a round-bladed knife. A soft, rough dough should form. You may need to add a little more milk to take up any remaining flour. Tip the dough out on to a lightly floured surface and knead very briefly to smooth it, then shape into a ball.

4. Place the dough in the centre of the prepared baking tray. Dust the dough with flour and, with floured hands, lightly flatten it into a 20–22cm (8–8½in) round, about 3cm (1¼in) thick. Dust a long, sharp knife with flour and cut the dough into 8 equal wedges. Spread out across the baking tray, then brush the tops with a little egg wash. Top each one with a rocket leaf, followed by a second layer of egg wash.

5. Bake for 20–25 minutes or until risen and golden brown. Serve warm from the oven, split in half, with a generous spread of butter. These scones are best eaten on the day of making, but will keep for up to 2 days in an airtight container – reheat them in the oven before serving.

I've been making this recipe for years, and it is a firm favourite; people always fight over the edges, which become crispy with bacon fat. I recently added sweetcorn kernels to the batter, which provide a juicy pop of sweetness. Slice into big wedges and serve up as part of a barbecue spread with plenty of butter.

Bacon and buttermilk cornbread

Serves 8 ~ Preparation time 15 minutes
Cooking time 20–25 minutes

4 smoked streaky bacon rashers
25g (1oz) salted butter, plus extra to serve
175g (6oz) cornmeal or polenta
100g (3½oz) plain flour
½ teaspoon baking powder
½ teaspoon bicarbonate of soda
½ teaspoon salt
285ml (9½fl oz) buttermilk
3 tablespoons maple syrup
2 large eggs, beaten
100g (3½oz) sweetcorn, canned or frozen (defrost if using frozen)

1. Preheat the oven to 220°C (200°C fan/425°F/gas mark 7).
2. Find a medium-sized frying pan (about 23cm/9in in diameter) with an ovenproof handle (see tip). Heat this over a medium heat and add the bacon rashers. Cook for 6–7 minutes until the bacon is crisp. Remove the bacon rashers from the pan and drain on kitchen paper, leaving the fat they've released in the pan. Turn off the heat, add the butter and allow it to melt.
3. In a large bowl, combine the cornmeal, flour, baking powder, bicarbonate of soda and salt. Make a well in the centre and pour in the buttermilk, 2 tablespoons of the maple syrup and the beaten eggs. Beat the ingredients together to form a thick batter, then fold in the sweetcorn. Finely chop the cooked bacon and fold three-quarters of it through the batter, then tip the bacon fat and butter mixture into the bowl and stir to combine.
4. Return the frying pan to the heat and, once hot, tip in the batter. Smooth the top with a spatula, sprinkle with the remaining bacon, then transfer to the oven and bake for 17–20 minutes, or until a skewer inserted into the middle comes out clean.
5. When the cornbread is ready, take it out of the oven and brush the top with the remaining maple syrup. Allow to cool slightly, then slice into wedges and serve with plenty of butter. This cornbread will keep for 2 days stored in an airtight container.

TIP
If you don't have an ovenproof frying pan, use a regular frying pan to cook the bacon and then bake the mixture in a 23cm (9in) round cake tin. Ensure you butter it thoroughly first to prevent the mixture sticking.

Yes, I'm that person: as soon as spring hits and I'm out on a country walk, you'll find me foraging the undergrowth searching for elusive patches of wild garlic, filling whatever pockets I've got available, then trundling home, reeking of garlic (much to the joy of my companions) but delighted with my finds. These tarts celebrate wild garlic, but can also be made with regular garlic when it isn't in season.

Mushroom and wild garlic spelt tarts

Makes 4 individual tarts ~ Preparation time 30 minutes, plus chilling ~ **Cooking time** 30–35 minutes

1 tablespoon olive oil
150g (5½oz) chestnut mushrooms, finely sliced
25g (1oz) kale, torn, woody stems removed
small bunch of wild garlic, torn, or 1 garlic clove, crushed
2 large eggs
140g (5oz) crème fraîche
70ml (scant 2½fl oz) double cream
125g (4½oz) mature Cheddar cheese, finely grated
freshly ground black pepper

FOR THE PASTRY
75g (2¾oz) wholemeal spelt flour (or regular wholemeal flour)
150g (5½oz) plain flour
125g (4½oz) salted butter, chilled and cubed
2–3 tablespoons water

You will need baking beans, or dried rice or lentils

1. To make the pastry, tip the flours and cubed butter into a food processor and pulse until the mixture resembles fine breadcrumbs. You can also do this step by hand, rubbing the butter into the flours in a large bowl. Add the water (you may not need it all) and stir to combine. When the mixture clumps together, knead briefly, then wrap in clingfilm and chill in the fridge for at least 30 minutes, or until required (the pastry will keep for up to 2 days at this stage).

2. Preheat the oven to 180°C (160°C fan/350°F/gas mark 4) and place 4 deep 10cm (4in) fluted tart tins on a baking tray. Divide the pastry into four equal pieces and shape each into a ball, then roll out and use it to line each tin, pressing with your fingertips so the pastry fits snugly into all the corners. Don't worry if there are holes; simply patch these up with any leftover pastry. Roll your rolling pin over the top to help trim any excess dough. Prick the bases with a fork, then line with baking parchment and fill with baking beans, rice or lentils. Blind-bake the tarts for 15 minutes, then remove the parchment and beans/rice/lentils and bake for a further 5 minutes until the bases feel crisp. Remove from the oven and set aside. Increase the oven temperature to 200°C (180°C fan/400°F/gas mark 6).

3. Meanwhile, heat the oil in a frying pan over a medium heat. Add the mushrooms and cook, stirring frequently, until they soften and start to become crisp. Add the kale and wild garlic (or crushed garlic), and cook for a further minute or so until tender. Divide the mixture between the tart tins.

continued overleaf...

4 Use a fork to beat the eggs in a measuring jug, then add the crème fraîche, cream and three-quarters of the Cheddar. Season with a crack of black pepper. Mix until well combined, then pour over the mushrooms in the pastry cases. Sprinkle the remaining cheese over the tops. Bake the tarts for 12–15 minutes, until the filling is set and the tops are golden brown. Allow to cool completely before removing from the tins. These tarts will keep for up to 3 days stored in the fridge.

TIP
Make them mini! Use a muffin tin to make miniature versions of these tarts – perfect to take on a picnic.

Don't be fooled, this is very much a herb salad with added bulgur, not the other way round. Traditional tabbouleh uses very fine bulgur wheat, but the coarse type will work here too. I chop the herbs by hand, to give the salad more body and save them from accidently being puréed! It's delicious served with romaine lettuce cups as makeshift spoons, and try sprinkling with pomegranate and feta for an extra treat.

Tabbouleh salad

Serves 4 as a side ~ Preparation time 20 minutes

50g (1¾oz) bulgur wheat
100g (3½oz) flat-leaf parsley (about 2 bunches)
25g (1oz) mint
1 large beef tomato, deseeded and finely diced
¼ cucumber, deseeded and finely diced
5 spring onions, finely diced
4 tablespoons extra virgin olive oil
zest and juice of 1 lemon
sea salt and freshly ground black pepper

1. Cook the bulgur wheat according to the packet instructions – if you've got fine bulgur wheat, this will simply need soaking in boiling water, while coarser bulgur requires boiling in a small saucepan until tender. Fluff the bulgur with a fork to separate the grains and let it cool to room temperature.

2. Use a sharp knife to finely chop the parsley and mint (or use a food processor if speed is of the essence) – the finer the better. Include the parsley stalks but discard the mint stalks, as these are too woody.

3. Combine the diced tomato, cucumber and spring onions in a large serving bowl. Add the chopped herbs and cooled bulgur wheat.

4. In a small bowl, whisk together the extra virgin olive oil and lemon zest and juice. Season with salt and pepper and pour this dressing over the prepared salad, tossing gently to combine. Taste and add more seasoning if needed, then serve immediately or pack into a container to take on a picnic or to a barbecue.

I often find bought coleslaw to be cloying and too heavy on the mayonnaise, but this is fresh and lively, with a jalapeño kick and salty mature Cheddar woven through it. Don't combine the shredded vegetables with the creamy dressing until you are ready to serve; this will keep things as crunchy as possible. You can prepare both in advance and keep chilled for up to 3 days, then mix together when needed.

Cheddar and jalapeño slaw

Serves 8 ~ Preparation time 15 minutes

½ red cabbage
½ white cabbage
2 carrots, peeled
large handful of coriander, chopped
2 green jalapeño peppers, deseeded and chopped
100g (3½oz) mature Cheddar cheese, coarsely grated

FOR THE DRESSING
50ml (2fl oz) olive oil
50g (1¾oz) mayonnaise
1 tablespoon apple cider vinegar
1 tablespoon caster sugar
1 teaspoon sea salt flakes

1. Remove and discard the core from both cabbages, then slice as thinly as possible using a sharp knife or a mandoline. Place the shredded cabbage in a large bowl. Use a peeler (or mandoline) to peel long strips from the carrot, then cut each strip into thin batons and add to the bowl with the cabbage.

2. To make the dressing, place all the ingredients in a small bowl. Mix well to combine.

3. When you're ready to serve, add the creamy dressing to the slaw, along with most of the chopped coriander, as well as the jalapeños and Cheddar. Mix thoroughly until completely coated, then sprinkle with the remaining coriander and serve.

This soup is a summer entertaining go-to, because: a) it makes the best of juicy, fragrant summer tomatoes when they are at their peak, and b) it requires minimal chopping and no stirring a hot pan, making it ideal for sticky days when cooking feels like too much! I make this soup in bulk with a glut of summer tomatoes, then freeze portions ready for chillier days when I want a burst of sunny warmth.

Summer tomato soup

Serves 4 ~ **Preparation time** 20 minutes
Cooking time 45 minutes

1.25kg (2lb 12 oz) mixed tomatoes, larger ones chopped, cherry tomatoes left whole
1 onion, chopped into wedges
5 garlic cloves, unpeeled
2 tablespoons olive oil
450ml (16fl oz) vegetable stock
sea salt and freshly ground black pepper
crème fraîche, to serve (optional)

FOR THE CROUTONS
2 thick slices of sourdough
1 garlic clove, halved
2 tablespoons olive oil

FOR THE BASIL OIL
25g (1oz) basil, leaves picked
zest of ½ lemon
70ml (scant 2½fl oz) extra virgin olive oil

1. Preheat the oven to 220°C (200°C fan/425°F/gas mark 7). Combine the tomatoes, onion wedges and garlic cloves in a large roasting tin. Drizzle generously with the olive oil and season well. Roast for 35 minutes until the tomatoes are soft and blistered.

2. Meanwhile, make the croutons by rubbing each piece of sourdough with half a garlic clove. Tear the bread into small pieces and arrange on a baking tray, then drizzle with the olive oil and bake for 10 minutes until crisp and dry.

3. Tip the roasted tomatoes and onion into a blender, along with any juices from the roasting tin. Squeeze the roasted garlic cloves out of their skins and add to the blender. Blitz until smooth, then add the vegetable stock and blend again, adding a little more until you reach your desired consistency. Season to taste, then chill until needed (this soup will keep for up to 3 days in the fridge, or up to 3 months in the freezer).

4. For the basil oil, whizz the basil leaves in a mini food processor, then add the lemon zest and olive oil and mix again. Alternatively, chop the leaves very finely using a sharp knife and mix with the lemon zest and olive oil in a bowl.

5. Warm the soup through, then serve in large bowls with swirls of herb oil, croutons and crème fraîche, if liked.

These crispy filo parcels stuffed with a herby spinach and feta filling are based on the Greek spanakopita pie. They make a comforting treat that is perfect for picnics, and can also be served as a great canapé or starter with seasoned Greek yogurt for dipping.

Spanakopita filo triangles

Makes 18 ~ Preparation time 25 minutes
Cooking time 20–25 minutes

1 tablespoon olive oil
2 garlic cloves, finely chopped
2 teaspoons ground cumin
250g (9oz) feta cheese
150g (5½oz) spinach, roughly chopped
small bunch of flat-leaf parsley, finely chopped
small bunch of mint, leaves picked and finely chopped
zest and juice of ½ lemon
1 large egg, beaten
75g (2¾oz) salted butter
270g (9½oz) pack filo pastry sheets (about 6 sheets)
2 teaspoons sesame seeds

1. Preheat the oven to 200°C (180°C fan/400°F/gas mark 6) and line a large baking tray with baking parchment.

2. Heat the olive oil in a small frying pan over a medium heat and add the chopped garlic. Fry for 1 minute until softened and starting to go brown, then stir in the cumin and remove from the heat.

3. Crumble the feta into a large bowl and add the fried garlic mixture, along with the chopped spinach, chopped herbs and lemon zest. Stir to combine, then add the lemon juice and the beaten egg and mix again until everything is properly mixed in.

4. Melt the butter in the pan you used to fry the garlic (don't worry if you get specks in the butter, they only add to the flavour).

5. Unroll the filo pastry pack so that all the sheets are directly on top of each other in a block. Slice the pastry lengthways into 3 rectangles, cutting through all the layers so you end up with 18 long strips in total.

6. To assemble the triangles, lay out a strip of pastry and brush with melted butter. Place a heaped teaspoon of spinach mixture in the bottom corner of the filo strip. Fold the pastry and filling over to create a small triangle containing the filling. Continue to flip the triangle across the pastry strip as if you are making a samosa, until the filling is completely wrapped and the pastry is used up. Repeat with the remaining filling and pastry strips.

7. Arrange the parcels on the baking tray and brush with any remaining melted butter. Sprinkle with the sesame seeds and bake for 20–25 minutes until golden brown. Allow to cool slightly before enjoying warm or at room temperature. These pastries will keep for up to 3 days stored in an airtight container.

The perfect dish to cart along to a bring-and-share lunch or beach picnic! Here, the summery flavours of Greek salad, complete with fresh herbs, meet tender new potatoes in a red wine vinegar and peppery olive oil dressing for a reinvented potato salad that you'll love.

Greek-style potato salad

Serves 4 ~ **Preparation time** 10 minutes, plus standing time
Cooking time 15–20 minutes

800g (1lb 12oz) new or baby potatoes
15 Kalamata olives, pitted and halved
100g (3½oz) sun-dried tomatoes
½ red onion, finely sliced
75g (2¾oz) feta cheese
sea salt and freshly ground black pepper

FOR THE DRESSING
½ teaspoon Dijon mustard
4 tablespoons extra virgin olive oil (I like to use Greek)
3 tablespoons red wine vinegar
1 garlic clove, finely grated
1 teaspoon dried oregano
20g (¾oz) dill, finely chopped
½ teaspoon sea salt flakes

1. Bring a large saucepan of salted water to the boil. Chop any large potatoes in half, then add to the water and boil for 15–20 minutes, or until tender. Drain and allow to cool completely.

2. To make the dressing, mix together the mustard, olive oil and red wine vinegar in a jug. Add the garlic and oregano, and stir vigorously to combine. Stir in the dill and season with the sea salt and a few cracks of freshly ground black pepper.

3. Tip the cooked potatoes into a serving bowl and add the olives, sun-dried tomatoes and red onion. Pour over the dressing, then toss to combine and coat each potato. Leave to stand for at least 15 minutes to allow the potatoes to absorb the dressing. Crumble over the feta just before serving. You can make this salad ahead of time and store it in a sealed container in the fridge for up to 3 days, adding the feta when you're ready to serve.

These lollies celebrate mangoes and all their juicy goodness. My sister served little shots of mango lassi with the canapés at her wedding, and they were so delicious I downed six or seven. These sweet and sunny lollies take me straight back to that joyful day. All mangoes have a slightly different level of sweetness, so give the mixture a taste and adjust the quantity of condensed milk accordingly.

Mango lassi lollies

Makes 6 lollies ~ Preparation time 10 minutes, plus freezing

seeds from 3 green cardamom pods (or ¼ teaspoon ground cardamom)
1 large ripe mango, ideally Alphonso (you need about 325g/11½oz flesh)
175g (6oz) full-fat Greek yogurt
75g (2¾oz) sweetened condensed milk, plus extra as needed
crushed pistachio dust (see Tips), to serve (optional)

You will need 6 × 100ml (3½fl oz) lolly moulds

1. Tip the cardamom seeds into a spice grinder and blitz until they are finely ground (or use a pestle and mortar).
2. Prepare the mango by discarding the stone and skin, then add the flesh a blender, along with the ground cardamom.
3. Add the yogurt and condensed milk, then blitz until completely smooth. Taste and add more condensed milk if you'd like your lollies sweeter.
4. Divide between your lolly moulds and freeze for at least 6 hours. Serve with pistachio dust to dip, if liked. These will keep for up to 3 months in the freezer.

TIP
To make pistachio dust, tip 50g (1¾oz) pistachio nuts into a spice grinder or mini food processor and blitz into dust, with just a few small nut pieces remaining. This will keep in an airtight glass jar or container for up to 2 weeks.

Soft, spicy cookies wrapped around caramel rippled no-churn ice cream: what's not to love? Trust me on the spices and pepper here – the flavours work really well. Slice into bars and wrap in baking parchment to take them on adventures in a cool bag.

Speculoos caramel ice-cream sandwiches

Makes 12 ice-cream sandwiches ~ **Preparation time** 25 minutes, plus freezing ~ **Cooking time** 15–17 minutes

FOR THE COOKIE DOUGH
140g (5oz) salted butter, softened, plus extra for greasing
120g (4¼oz) soft dark brown sugar
100g (3½oz) caster sugar
1 teaspoon vanilla extract
1 large egg
250g (9oz) plain flour
½ teaspoon bicarbonate of soda
½ teaspoon baking powder
1 teaspoon mixed spice
¼ teaspoon ground ginger
½ teaspoon ground cinnamon
¼ teaspoon ground white pepper

FOR THE ICE CREAM
200g (7oz) condensed milk
600ml (20fl oz) double cream
1 teaspoon vanilla bean paste
125g (4½oz) shop-bought salted caramel sauce

1. Preheat the oven to 190°C (170°C fan/375°F/gas mark 5). Grease two 20 × 30cm (8 × 12in) lipped baking trays with butter and line with baking parchment.

2. In a large bowl, beat together the softened butter with both the sugars using a wooden spoon until they are well combined. Add the vanilla extract and egg before beating again until all the ingredients are smooth.

3. In a separate bowl, combine the flour, bicarbonate of soda, baking powder and spices. Pour the dry ingredients into the wet mixture and fold using a spatula until a stiff dough forms.

4. Divide the cookie dough in half, then tip each half into one of the prepared tins and use the heel of your hand to press the dough into an even layer, making sure to get right to the edges.

5. Bake for 14–16 minutes, or until the cookie dough begins to brown and become crispy around the edges. the top should look crisp but will feel soft and undercooked when pressed; this is ideal. Remove from the oven and allow to cool completely in the tins.

6. To make the ice cream, line a deeper 20 × 30cm (8 × 12in) baking tray with clingfilm or baking parchment. In a large bowl, whisk together the condensed milk, double cream and vanilla bean paste using an electric whisk until the mixture thickens and holds its shape when you take the whisk out. Lift the cookie dough sheets off their trays and invert one of them into the new lined tin. Spread the ice-cream mixture over the top of the cookie sheet, then dollop over the salted caramel sauce and briefly swirl together using the back of a knife. Sandwich with the second sheet of cookie, placing it top-side up.

7   Freeze for at least 4 hours, or until firm. Use a sharp knife to slice into rectangles, then serve the ice-cream sandwiches immediately, or individually wrap and take out in a cool box. They will also keep in the freezer for up to 3 months, if you're not planning to serve them all on the day of making. To freeze, wrap each sandwich in baking parchment and store them in an airtight container.

Weekend table

A day-and-night-long project, but worth it. I spent weeks developing this focaccia recipe, striking the balance between an artisan slow-fermented bread with bubbles galore, and something achievable at home and hands-off enough to become a staple. The stretching and folding may sound complicated, but once you've got the hang of it, it is very straightforward – and far less messy than traditional kneading.

Overnight focaccia

Makes 1 large loaf ~ **Preparation time** 20 minutes, plus resting and proving ~ **Cooking time** 20–25 minutes

500g (1lb 2oz) strong white bread flour
7g sachet (2 teaspoons) fast-action dried yeast
1 teaspoon caster sugar
2 teaspoons table salt
3 tablespoons olive oil, plus extra for greasing and to serve
400ml (14fl oz) lukewarm water
1 rosemary sprig, leaves picked
1 teaspoon sea salt flakes, to sprinkle
balsamic vinegar, to serve

1. Sift the flour, yeast, sugar and salt into a large mixing bowl and mix well to combine. Combine 2 tablespoons of the olive oil with the lukewarm water, then stir into the flour mixture to create a very wet, sticky dough; you're just looking to briefly combine the ingredients so no floury streaks remain. Cover the bowl with a clean tea towel and leave to rest for 20 minutes. This will allow the gluten to relax and prepare the dough for stretching and folding.

2. Now we are going to perform four stretch-and-fold motions: at the top and bottom, and to the left and right of the dough. Wet your fingers with water, then scoop and grip the edge of the dough at the top of the bowl. Stretch the dough vertically, then fold over the ball of dough, completely covering it with the stretched piece. Rotate the bowl 90 degrees and repeat the stretch-and-fold motion three more times, rotating the bowl 90 degrees each time. You'll end up with a parcel of dough. It won't look smooth at this point, but it will once it has finished rising.

3. Cover and leave to rise for 3–5 hours, repeating the stretch-and-fold process three more times. Try to space your stretch and folds evenly over the rising time, but don't stress too much, as the dough is very forgiving. By the final time, the dough will look smooth and uniform, and will jiggle when you shake the bowl. It should also have doubled in size.

4. Prepare a 23 × 30cm (9 × 12in) lipped baking tray by drizzling it with about 1 tablespoon of olive oil. Tip the risen dough on to the tray, coat it in the oil and then use oiled fingertips to spread the dough right out to the edges. If the dough refuses to spread, leave it on the tray for 20 minutes and then try again when the gluten has relaxed. Cover the tray, ideally with a reusable plastic bag, and refrigerate overnight, or for 8–12 hours.

continued overleaf...

5. In the morning, remove the tray from the fridge and allow the dough to come to room temperature (this usually takes 2 hours). The tray should no longer feel cool to the touch and the dough should be jiggly when shaken.

6. Preheat the oven to 230°C (210°C fan/450°F/gas mark 8) and place an empty baking tin on the bottom rack of the oven. Oil your fingertips and drizzle the dough with the remaining 1 tablespoon of olive oil, then dimple the dough all over, leaving recesses where your fingers have been and creating beautiful bubbles. Push the rosemary into some of these holes, then sprinkle the top of the focaccia generously with sea salt flakes.

7. Pour a large mugful of water into the preheated baking tin in the oven to create steam, and place the focaccia in the centre of the oven. Bake for 20–25 minutes, until golden brown all over.

8. Allow to cool in the tin for 5 minutes, then transfer to a wire rack to cool completely (if you let it cool completely in the tin, the bottom of the loaf will become soggy). Cut into large squares and serve with olive oil and balsamic vinegar for dipping. This focaccia is best eaten on the day of making, but if you do have any leftovers, warm them up in a low oven to refresh.

FOCACCIA TOPPING IDEAS

Potato and rosemary
Slice 400g (14oz) new potatoes as thinly as possible, then toss with 1 tablespoon of olive oil and season with salt and pepper. Layer over the top of the risen dough, stud with rosemary and bake for 5 minutes longer than above to ensure the potato is cooked through.

Za'atar, feta cheese and pine nut
Sprinkle the risen dough with 2 tablespoons of za'atar, 75g (2¾oz) of crumbled feta and 50g (1¾oz) of pine nuts before baking as above.

Cherry tomato, olive and caper
Stud the risen dough with 150g (5½oz) of halved cherry tomatoes, cut-sides up, 50g (1¾oz) of black olives and 2 tablespoons of capers before baking as above.

I cook a huge variety of different things, so when my family can vividly remember a dish, I know it's a good 'un! This is one such dish: juicy, tender, herb-infused pork with salt-crusted crackling. I find it much easier to get hold of pork belly than a traditional porchetta cut, which has the ribs removed but the loin attached. Serve with gravy and roast potatoes, or with salad and buttered rolls.

Crispy fennel, orange and garlic porchetta

Serves 8–10 ~ **Preparation time** 30 minutes
Cooking time 3–4 hours

2 tablespoons sea salt flakes, plus extra to season the skin
1 teaspoon cracked black pepper
1 tablespoon fennel seeds
6 garlic cloves
small bunch of flat-leaf parsley, finely chopped
small bunch of oregano, finely chopped
zest and juice of ½ orange
zest and juice of ½ lemon
2 tablespoons olive oil
2.5–3kg (5lb 8oz–6lb 8oz) pork belly, skin on, ideally with skin scored by the butcher
3 carrots, halved lengthways
1 fennel bulb, cut lengthways into 3 even pieces
300ml (10fl oz) white wine (or water)

1 Grind together the sea salt flakes, black pepper and fennel seeds using a pestle and mortar (or an electric spice grinder or mini food processor) until finely ground. Add the garlic cloves, herbs, orange and lemon zest and juice and 1 tablespoon of the olive oil, then pound or blitz again until a rough paste forms.

2 If the pork belly hasn't been scored, use a sharp knife (I find a craft knife or penknife most successful for this) to score the skin in roughly 2cm (¾in) intervals across, then pat it dry using kitchen paper. Flip the pork over, skin side down, and turn it so the shorter end is facing you. Butterfly the pork belly, cutting from the outside and opening it like a book, leaving it attached on the far side. This should double the surface area of your pork.

continued overleaf...

3. Spread the herby filling mixture over the pork, massaging it into all the exposed flesh. Fold one side back in to the centre, and leave one flap open. Starting at the opened side of your butterflied piece of meat, begin to tightly roll up the meat into a neat joint. The skin should almost come together under the pork, but shouldn't become part of the roll or it will become chewy, so trim away any additional rind.

4. Lay 8–10 lengths of butcher's twine under the pork and tie tightly to secure the roll. If you want to get ahead, at this stage you can place the meat in the fridge, uncovered, for up to 24 hours, until you're ready to cook.

5. Preheat the oven to 250°C (230°C fan/485°F/gas mark 9½). Arrange the carrots and fennel in the base of a deep roasting tin. Lay the pork on top and massage the skin with the remaining olive oil, then sprinkle generously with sea salt flakes.

6. Roast the porchetta for 30 minutes, then reduce the oven temperature to 180°C (160°C fan/350°F/gas mark 4). Add the wine or water to the base of the pan, then cook for a further 2½–3 hours, until the centre of the pork registers at least 75°C (165°F) on a meat thermometer. Turn the heat to 250°C (230°C fan/485°F/gas mark 9½) for the final 15 minutes of cooking to crisp the skin, keeping a close eye on it. If the crackling hasn't reached your desired level of crispness, try placing the joint under a hot grill until the crackling is suitably bubbled and golden.

7. Allow the joint to rest for at least 20 minutes before slicing thinly with a serrated knife to serve.

TIP

This recipe makes a large porchetta joint, perfect for a crowd or for delicious leftovers. You can also scale down the recipe for a smaller joint of pork belly – it needs around 30 minutes per 500g (1lb 2oz) at 180°C (160°C fan/350°F/gas mark 4) after the initial 30-minute hot blast.

I believe that if you're going to bother with deep-frying, you might as well fry everything! Essentially translating as 'fried mixed', fritto misto transports me to the Amalfi coast, and the joys of a glass of rosé and a plate of fried seafood. This makes a great dinner-party starter. I've gone with courgette and seafood, but you can use this batter to coat whatever you'd like to fry; try it with broccoli or even mushrooms.

Black pepper fritto misto

Serves 6 as a starter ~ **Preparation time** 10 minutes
Cooking time 15 minutes

vegetable oil, for deep-frying
25g (1oz) plain flour
150g (5½oz) raw peeled king prawns
165g (5¾oz) raw squid, cleaned, tubes sliced into thick rings and tentacles left whole
1 courgette (yellow or green), sliced into half-moons 1cm (½in) thick
small bunch of sage, leaves picked
lemon wedges, to serve

FOR THE BATTER
90g (3¼oz) plain flour
90g (3¼oz) cornflour
½ teaspoon baking powder
1 teaspoon cracked black pepper
¼ teaspoon fine sea salt, plus extra to serve
200ml (6¾fl oz) sparkling water or soda water

1. Pour oil into a large, heavy-based saucepan or cast-iron pot to a depth of 6cm (2½in). Place over a medium heat and heat the oil until it registers 180°C (350°F) on a thermometer. If you don't have a thermometer, test the oil by adding a small cube of bread – it should take 30–40 seconds to brown.

2. Meanwhile, make the batter. Combine the plain flour, cornflour, baking powder, black pepper and salt in a medium mixing bowl. Make a well in the centre, then add the sparkling or soda water and whisk until a smooth batter forms (don't worry if there are a few small lumps).

3. Tip the 25g (1oz) of plain flour into a shallow dish and coat the prawns and squid in a light dusting of flour; this will help the batter to stick. Dip the prawns in the batter, allowing any excess to drip back into the bowl, then carefully add to the hot oil and cook, stirring occasionally to stop the pieces sticking together, until the coating is crisp and cooked through – this will take 2–3 minutes. Use a slotted spoon to transfer to a tray lined with kitchen paper to absorb any excess oil. Repeat this process to fry the squid, followed by the courgette. Finally, dip the sage leaves in the batter and fry in the same way – they will take 1–2 minutes. The oil temperature will decrease as you add the different ingredients, so monitor it closely, making sure it remains at around 180°C (350°F) and adjusting the heat as necessary.

4. When everything is ready, sprinkle the fritto misto with sea salt and serve straight away on a big platter with fresh lemon wedges for squeezing.

TIP
If you're feeding a mixed group of plant- and seafood-eaters, dip and fry the vegetables first, so the batter and oil don't become contaminated.

139

Brisket is a hugely undervalued cut of beef. It needs slow cooking to become tender and shreddable – it's particularly delicious when braised in rich spices and sweet pomegranate. I discovered vermicelli rice in Lebanon, and love the contrasting texture of the toasted soft noodles with gently salted rice. This recipe uses a low oven, but you could use a slow cooker: simply cook on low for 8 hours.

Sticky pomegranate brisket with vermicelli rice

Serves 4–6 ~ Preparation time 25 minutes
Cooking time 3½–4 hours

1–1.25kg (2lb 4oz–2lb 12oz) rolled beef brisket
2 tablespoons olive oil
2 red onions, sliced into wedges
3 garlic cloves, finely chopped
1 teaspoon ground cinnamon
1 teaspoon ground coriander
1 teaspoon sweet paprika
375ml (13fl oz) pomegranate juice
5 tablespoons light soy sauce
50ml (2fl oz) pomegranate molasses
2 tablespoons tomato purée
sea salt flakes and freshly ground black pepper

FOR THE VERMICELLI RICE
320g (11¼oz) basmati rice
2 tablespoons olive oil
50g (1¾oz) vermicelli noodles, broken into short strands
750ml (3 cups) water
½ teaspoon salt

TO SERVE
seeds from 1 pomegranate
freshly chopped flat-leaf parsley
2 tablespoons toasted pine nuts (optional)
flatbreads (optional)

1. Preheat the oven to 160°C (140°C fan/325°F/gas mark 3).

2. Unroll the beef brisket, discarding any string used to tie it together, then slice in half or thirds, so the pieces will fit roughly into one layer in a large cast-iron casserole dish without overlapping too much.

3. Heat half the olive oil over a medium–high heat in the empty casserole dish, then add the first piece of meat. Allow it to caramelize and brown for a few minutes on each side, then set aside on a plate and repeat with the remaining meat.

4. Once the meat has been seared all over, add the onion to the now-empty pan, along with the remaining oil, and reduce the heat to medium. Cook, stirring often, for 4–5 minutes until the onion is beginning to soften, then add the chopped garlic and cook for a further 2 minutes. Add the spices and mix well to coat.

5. In a measuring jug, mix together the pomegranate juice, soy sauce, pomegranate molasses and tomato purée. Pour this into the casserole dish and bring to a simmer, then add the beef pieces, pushing them down into the liquid so they are mostly covered. Season with salt and pepper, then put the lid on and place the dish in the oven. Roast for 3½–4 hours, or until the meat is tender enough to be shredded using two forks.

continued overleaf...

6   Meanwhile, to make the vermicelli rice, rinse the rice in a sieve under running water until it runs clear. Heat the olive oil in a large saucepan and add the vermicelli. Fry the pasta strands, stirring all the time, until they turn a golden brown colour. Add the rice, stir well to coat, then pour in the measured water and add the salt. Reduce the heat to the lowest setting, cover the pan with a lid and cook for 15 minutes, then turn off the heat. Allow the vermicelli rice to sit, covered, for 5 minutes, before fluffing with a fork.

7   Once the meat is cooked, remove it from the casserole dish using tongs, place on a large serving plate or board, and cover with foil to rest for 10 minutes. Meanwhile, simmer the sauce until it is reduced and slightly thickened.

8   Shred the rested beef into long strands using two forks, then return it to the sauce. Toss well to combine, then arrange on a serving plate and sprinkle with fresh pomegranate seeds and a scattering of fresh parsley.

9   Serve with the vermicelli rice, topped with toasted pine nuts, if using, and some Lebanese-style flatbreads, if you wish.

When you make these crispy golden sticks of delight, you have to promise me not to be stingy with the Parmesan! You can never have enough: the concentrated umami taste of the cheese takes the chips to a whole new level, so be generous.

Baked polenta chips

Serves 4 as a starter or 2 as a side ~ Preparation time 10 minutes, plus chilling ~ **Cooking time** 25–30 minutes

550ml (19fl oz) chicken or vegetable stock
175g (6oz) quick-cook polenta
75g (2¾oz) Parmesan cheese, freshly grated
½ teaspoon cracked black pepper
2 tablespoons olive oil

1. Heat the stock in a medium-sized saucepan over a medium heat until simmering, then whisk in the polenta. Cook for 5–6 minutes, stirring all the time, until the mixture is thick and beginning to pull away from the sides of the pan. Add half the grated Parmesan and the black pepper, then mix well until melted.

2. Line a small baking tray or rectangular dish with baking parchment. Tip the cooked polenta into the prepared tray and spread into an even layer, gently compressing it with a spatula. Cover and chill for at least 1 hour (or up to 2 days) until firm.

3. When you're ready to cook, preheat the oven to 200°C (180°C fan/400°F/gas mark 6) and line a large baking tray with baking parchment. Tip the set block of polenta on to a chopping board and slice into thick chip shapes, approximately 2 x 5cm (¾ x 2in). Brush each chip with a little olive oil, then arrange on the baking tray and bake for 25–30 minutes, gently turning halfway through to ensure even crispness.

4. Once crisp and golden brown, remove from the oven and top with the remaining grated Parmesan. Allow it to melt over the chips, then place in a bowl and serve piping hot.

Earl Grey tea has a slight smokiness, and is aromatic and zesty with bergamot oil – both characteristics that complement the richness of fresh salmon. Marinating the fish in tea and citrus zest creates a unique flavour that is sure to get your guests talking! Loose-leaf tea is best here, but tea bags will work if you don't have any to hand. I like to serve this with fresh green salad and crusty bread or potatoes.

Earl Grey roast salmon

Serves 4–6 ~ Preparation time 10 minutes, plus marinating
Cooking time 20–25 minutes

2 tablespoons loose-leaf Earl Grey tea (or 3 teabags)
250ml (9fl oz) boiling water
zest of 1 orange
1 lemon, zested and sliced
2 teaspoons sea salt flakes
side of salmon, skin on (about 800g/1lb 12oz)
1 tablespoon olive oil
½ teaspoon soft light brown sugar

1 For the marinade, brew the loose-leaf tea or 2 of the teabags in the measured hot water for 4–5 minutes. Strain into a shallow container that is large enough to fit your salmon fillet and set the soaked tea leaves to one side (discard the teabags). Allow the tea to cool to room temperature, then add half the orange zest, half the lemon zest and 1 teaspoon of the sea salt flakes. Stir until the salt has dissolved, then lay the salmon in the marinade, skin-side up. Chill and allow the flavours to penetrate for at least 1 hour and up to 12 hours.

2 Preheat the oven to 200°C (180°C fan/400°F/gas mark 6). Line a baking tray with baking parchment or foil and drizzle with half a tablespoon of the olive oil. Remove the salmon from the marinade, allowing any excess to drip off, and place on the prepared baking tray, skin-side down.

3 In a small bowl, combine the remaining citrus zest and sea salt flakes with the brown sugar. Add 2 tablespoons of the reserved soaked tea leaves (or half the contents of the remaining dry teabag), then massage this mixture over the flesh of the salmon. Drizzle with the remaining olive oil, then arrange the lemon slices across the top of the salmon.

4 Roast for 20–25 minutes, until the salmon is cooked through, opaque and flakes away when pressed with a knife. Serve hot or cold, with your chosen accompaniments.

My mum's roast chicken will have me galivanting halfway across the country. When I asked her for the recipe, she was embarrassed by the simplicity, but if it turns out a perfect chicken, I'm here for it! The secret to the crispy skin feels counterintuitive: no oil. Let the fats from the poultry do all the crisping for you. Buy a higher-welfare chicken – with a recipe this simple, the quality of the ingredients really matters.

Mum's roast chicken

Serves 4–6 ~ Preparation time 10 minutes
Cooking time 1 hour 20 minutes

1 large higher-welfare chicken (around 1.5kg/3lb 5oz)
1 lemon, halved
6 garlic cloves
3 rosemary sprigs
3 lemon thyme sprigs
sea salt and freshly ground black pepper

1. Remove the chicken from the fridge 30 minutes before you are ready to cook and place in a large roasting tin. Preheat the oven to 220°C (200°C fan/425°F/gas mark 7).

2. Stuff the lemon halves into the chicken cavity, along with the garlic cloves and whole sprigs of rosemary and lemon thyme. Truss the chicken using a piece of butcher's twine, leaving the wings loose but tying the legs together. Pat the skin dry with a sheet of kitchen paper, then sprinkle liberally with salt and pepper.

3. Roast the chicken in the centre of the oven, rotating the tray once halfway to ensure an even cook, for around 1 hour 20 minutes (reduce or increase this time if your chicken is larger or smaller). When the chicken is cooked, it should be a deep golden brown all over, and a meat thermometer inserted into the thickest part of the legs and breast registers at least 75°C (165°F). Cover the bird with foil during cooking if you feel it is colouring too quickly.

4. Allow the chicken to rest, covered loosely with foil, for at least 20 minutes, before carving and serving. You can use all the ingredients you used to stuff the cavity, along with the meat juices and a splash of chicken stock and white wine, to make a gravy, if you like. Add a little cornflour mixed with water to thicken to your desired consistency and strain well before serving.

TIP
Save the crispy bits from the chicken drippings (also known as gribenes) that you find at the bottom of your roasting dish and use to make my Herby Yorkshire Puddings (see opposite).

Few foods bring me as much joy as a Yorkshire pudding. Watching the batter sizzle in the oil before inflating into puffy, golden clouds is the kind of kitchen magic that has me sitting cross-legged on the floor in front of the oven. Yorkshires aren't traditionally served with roast chicken, but I firmly believe every roast is improved by their addition – particularly if you add the crispy rendered chicken fat to the batter.

Herby Yorkshire puddings

Makes 12 large Yorkshire puddings ~ **Preparation time** 10 minutes, plus resting ~ **Cooking time** 20–25 minutes

4 large eggs
140g (5oz) plain flour
230ml (8fl oz) semi-skimmed milk
1 tablespoon chopped thyme leaves
olive oil, for the muffin tray
crispy chicken drippings (gribenes), from a roast chicken (optional, see opposite)
sea salt flakes and freshly ground black pepper

1. Whisk the eggs together in a large bowl, then add the flour and beat until a smooth paste has formed. Pour in the milk, a little at a time, still mixing continuously, until you have a runny batter about the consistency of double cream. Season with salt and pepper and add the thyme, then cover and chill until you're ready to bake (ideally for at least 2 hours).

2. Remove the batter from the fridge 30 minutes before use. Preheat the oven to 230°C (210°C fan/450°F/gas mark 8) and measure out 1 teaspoon of oil into each hole in a 12-muffin tray. Place the tray in the oven for 10 minutes to heat up.

3. If using, scrape the crispy dark brown pieces of rendered chicken fat off the base of the tin from a roast chicken (you want the solid parts, not the liquid fat). Roughly chop and add to the Yorkshire pudding batter, stirring to combine. Remove the muffin tray from the oven and quickly divide the batter between the holes – it may sizzle and spit in the oil, so be careful. Return to the oven and bake for 20–25 minutes, or until the puddings are risen and golden brown. Try not to open the oven during the cooking time, or the puddings may deflate.

4. Once they're ready, pop the Yorkshires out of the tin within a few minutes to prevent them from absorbing excess oil, then serve hot with plenty of gravy.

I truly believe that I reached my husband's heart partly through my potato dauphinoise. How can you not fall in love with this gratin (or the person cooking it)? Authentic versions do not contain cheese, so purists can leave it out, but I find that cheese only enhances the majestic nature of these creamy potatoes. I've suggested a nutty French Comté, but Gruyère or Parmesan will also work well.

Potato dauphinoise

Serves 6 ~ Preparation time 20 minutes
Cooking time 1 hour

300ml (10fl oz) double cream
300ml (10fl oz) whole milk
3 large garlic cloves, finely grated
generous grating of nutmeg
3 thyme sprigs
1 rosemary sprig
1kg (2lb 4oz) Maris Piper potatoes
25g (1oz) salted butter, softened
100g (3½oz) Comté cheese (or other Alpine hard cheese), grated
sea salt flakes and freshly ground black pepper

1. Preheat the oven to 200°C (180°C fan/400°F/gas mark 6).

2. Pour the cream and milk into a small saucepan over a low heat. Add the garlic, a few grinds of black pepper, a generous grating of nutmeg, and the thyme and rosemary sprigs. Bring to a simmer, then turn off the heat and allow to infuse for 15 minutes.

3. While you wait for the milk to infuse, peel the potatoes, then slice into thin discs using a mandoline, a food processor with a slicing attachment or a sharp knife.

4. When the milk is ready, remove and discard the herbs, and season with a pinch of sea salt flakes.

5. Grease a large (28 × 33cm/11 × 13in) ceramic baking dish with the butter. Set aside a third of the cheese for the top. Fill the dish by layering the potato slices, the remaining grated cheese and the infused cream, then repeating until all the potato slices are used up – aim for 4 or 5 layers of potatoes. Pour any remaining cream over the top, then sprinkle with the reserved cheese.

6. Bake the dauphinoise for 50 minutes–1 hour, covering with foil midway through if the top looks too brown. Allow to stand for 5 minutes, then serve immediately.

Your classic Sunday veg gets a nutty glow-up! Roasting vegetables is my favourite way to bring out their complexity of flavour, and coating sweet carrots in honey, sea salt flakes and pistachios transforms them into an impressive side dish you'll be proud to have grace your table.

Pistachio-crusted roasted carrots

Serves 6 as a side ~ Preparation time 10 minutes
Cooking time 40 minutes

600g (1lb 5oz) baby carrots, peeled and trimmed but with the tops attached, or regular carrots, peeled and cut into long batons
2 tablespoons olive oil
½ teaspoon sea salt flakes
2 teaspoons runny honey
50g (1¾oz) pistachio nuts, finely chopped

1. Preheat the oven to 220°C (200°C fan/425°F/gas mark 7). Place the carrots in a large roasting tin and drizzle with the olive oil. Sprinkle with the sea salt flakes and make sure everything is well coated.

2. Bake for 30 minutes, turning once halfway through the cooking, until the carrots are caramelized and soft.

3. Remove the carrots from the oven, drizzle with the honey and sprinkle with the chopped pistachio nuts. Toss well, then return to the oven for a further 10 minutes. Serve hot, or allow to cool and toss through salads.

WEEKEND TABLE

A friend told me about a man who lived above the coffee shop she worked in, who would buy a double espresso, then use it as the secret ingredient in bolognese sauce. I was sceptical, but after testing many variations, I'm blown away by the depth of flavour it brings. You can serve this with shop-bought pappardelle or spaghetti, but I recommend making your own pasta. Don't worry – handmade rusticity is fine!

Coffee bolognese with homemade pappardelle

Serves 4 ~ Preparation time 30 minutes
Cooking time 1 hour 30 minutes

1 tablespoon olive oil
100g (3½oz) smoked pancetta, diced
1 large onion, chopped
1 celery stick, chopped
1 carrot, grated
200g (7oz) chestnut mushrooms
500g (1lb 2oz) beef mince (10 per cent fat)
1 beef stock cube
400g (14oz) can chopped tomatoes
5 tablespoons strong coffee (such as espresso)
150ml (5fl oz) whole milk
1 bay leaf
sea salt flakes and freshly ground black pepper
Parmigiano Reggiano cheese, grated, to serve

FOR THE HOMEMADE PAPPARDELLE
400g (14oz) '00' pasta flour, plus extra for dusting
4 large eggs
semolina flour, for rolling

1. Warm the olive oil in a large saucepan over a high heat, then add the pancetta. Cook for 2–3 minutes until the pancetta is crisp and the fat has rendered down. Add the onion, celery and carrot. Sauté for 10–15 minutes, or until softened.

2. Finely chop the mushrooms, or blitz them briefly in a food processor to break them down into small pieces. Add to the pan, then crumble in the mince and stir, breaking up any large chunks using a wooden spoon, until browned all over.

3. Crumble in the stock cube, then add the tomatoes, coffee, milk and bay leaf. Stir well, cover with a lid and simmer on the lowest heat setting for at least 1 hour. The longer you simmer, the more intense and complex the flavour becomes. Continue to simmer until the liquid has reduced almost completely. Season to taste and remove the bay leaf.

4. While the sauce is reducing, make the pasta. Add the flour to the bowl of a food processor, then break in the eggs. Use the pulse function to blend for a few seconds at a time until a crumbly dough forms. Tip the dough on to a lightly floured surface and knead for a couple of minutes until a smooth, elastic dough forms (add a little water or extra flour if your dough is too crumbly or too soft). Alternatively, make the pasta in a mixing bowl by tipping the flour in first and cracking the eggs into a well in the centre. Use a fork to gradually mix the flour into the eggs until a dough forms, then knead as above.

5   Wrap the dough in clingfilm and let it rest at room temperature for about 30 minutes before dividing it into quarters. Dust your work surface with semolina flour and use a rolling pin to roll out one part as thinly as you can (alternatively, use a pasta machine).

6   Dust the pasta sheet with semolina flour, then roll it up and use a sharp knife to slice it into strips roughly 2cm (¾in) wide. Unroll each strip, shape into a nest and set aside before repeating with the remaining pasta dough. The pasta can sit for up to 2 hours before being cooked.

7   When ready to serve, bring a large pan of salted water to the boil. Carefully add the pappardelle, gently stirring to prevent sticking. Cook until al dente, usually about 3–5 minutes. Drain, reserving a small amount of cooking water in a mug, then add the pasta to the sauce and mix well. Add a splash of the pasta water to loosen the sauce so it coats each piece of pasta. Divide between shallow bowls and serve with lots of freshly grated Parmigiano Reggiano.

Pulled pork has taken the world by storm, and quite frankly, I'm not surprised! The secret to my pulled pork is to slow-cook it in pineapple juice. The fruit's acidity helps to tenderize the meat as it cooks, making it even easier to pull, and also imparts a delicious sweet-and-sour flavour which is perfect with pork.

Pineapple pulled pork tacos

Serves 6–8 ~ Preparation time 20 minutes, plus overnight marinating if possible ~ **Cooking time** 2½–3 hours

1 teaspoon cayenne pepper
1 teaspoon ground cinnamon
2 teaspoons paprika
1 tablespoon sea salt flakes
1 tablespoon soft dark brown sugar
1.5kg (3lb 5oz) pork shoulder
2 garlic cloves, finely chopped
1 tablespoon chipotle paste
500ml (18fl oz) pineapple juice
250ml (9fl oz) water

FOR THE CHARRED PINEAPPLE SALSA
1 fresh pineapple, peeled, cored and sliced into fingers
½ red onion, finely sliced
1 red chilli, sliced
small bunch of mint, leaves picked and finely chopped
2 teaspoons apple cider vinegar

TO SERVE
small soft tacos
freshly chopped coriander

1. The day before you are planning to cook the pork, prepare the rub. Mix together the spices, salt and sugar in a small bowl.

2. Remove any fat or skin from the outside of the pork and discard (or save the skin to make crackling!). Slice the joint into 3–4 equal-sized chunks, slicing on the diagonal along the grain to keep the meat strands as long as possible. Place in a large bowl, sprinkle over the rub and use your hands to massage it into the meat. Once completely coated, cover and chill overnight to allow the flavours to soak in. If you are in a rush, you can skip the marinating and cook the meat straight after rubbing, but the flavours won't be so intense.

3. Preheat the oven to 180°C (160°C fan/350°F/gas mark 4). Transfer the pork into a large cast-iron casserole dish with a lid and sprinkle over any of the rub that didn't stick to the meat. Add the garlic and chipotle paste, then pour over the pineapple juice and the water. The liquid should come roughly three-quarters of the way up the sides of the pork – add a little more water if it doesn't.

4. Cover with the lid and transfer to the oven. Cook for 2½–3 hours, checking every hour or so to monitor the liquid levels. Once the pork is ready, it should be tender and soft, with the liquid reduced to a thick and glossy sauce. You may need to remove the pork and simmer the sauce on the hob to reduce it down if it hasn't thickened enough during the cooking process.

continued overleaf...

5   Meanwhile, make the charred pineapple salsa. Heat a large frying pan over a medium–high heat. Add the pineapple fingers to the pan and cook for 3–4 minutes on each side, until a nice char develops. Remove and allow to cool to room temperature. Dice the charred pineapple and add to a bowl, along with the red onion, red chilli, mint and apple cider vinegar. Mix well.

6   When the pork is ready, use two forks to shred the meat and mix well with the sauce until it is well coated. At this point, you can serve or allow it to cool to room temperature and chill for up to 2 days. Serve the pineapple salsa alongside the pork, piled into soft tacos and sprinkled with coriander.

TIP
I love making this dish using a pressure cooker when I'm shorter on time, or in peak summer when I don't want the oven on for so long. Omit the 250ml (9fl oz) of water and cook the pork in a pressure cooker (hob or electric), for 35 minutes at high pressure. Allow the pressure to release naturally, then remove the pork and shred it. Simmer the liquid, uncovered, until it becomes a thick sauce.

My Italian friends may raise an eyebrow, but I love deep-pan pizza. Making it in an American-style sheet pan or large baking tray is a great way to feed a crowd, so this is a go-to party dish when we have friends round for a few drinks or to watch the football. Double up the dough quantity if you like, and mix up the toppings to suit your guests. Pepperoni and a drizzle of honey is our favourite!

Sheet-pan pizza

Serves 6 ~ Preparation time 20 minutes, plus resting and overnight proving ~ **Cooking time** 25–30 minutes

FOR THE DOUGH
350g (12oz) strong white bread flour
7g sachet (2 teaspoons) fast-action dried yeast
1 teaspoon table salt
260ml (8¾fl oz) water
olive oil, for greasing

FOR THE SAUCE
1 tablespoon olive oil
2 garlic cloves, finely chopped
200ml (7fl oz) passata
2 tablespoons tomato purée
1 teaspoon dried basil
½ teaspoon table salt
1 teaspoon caster sugar

FOR THE TOPPING
2 × 125g (4½oz) mozzarella balls, drained, patted dry and torn
50g (1¾oz) pepperoni or chorizo slices
1 tablespoon honey, to drizzle

1. To make the dough, combine the bread flour, yeast and salt in the bowl of a stand mixer. Add the water and mix until a soft, sticky dough forms. Knead using the dough hook attachment for 5 minutes, until the dough is stretchy and pliable. (You can also do this by hand, by mixing together the ingredients in a large bowl and kneading for 10 minutes, but the dough is high hydration, so will be trickier to manage.)

2. Grease a large rectangular plastic or glass container with oil, then place the dough in the container and cover with the lid or a clean tea towel for 30 minutes. Once the 30 minutes are up, wet your fingers and perform four 'stretch-and-fold' motions. To do this, tuck your fingers under the dough, stretch it upwards and then fold it over the remaining dough, then rotate the container 90 degrees and repeat until you have stretched and folded the dough on all four sides. This process develops the light structure of the dough.

3. Allow the dough to rise for a further 30 minutes, then repeat the stretch-and-fold process once more, before leaving the dough to rise for a further 30 minutes.

continued overleaf...

4   Oil a large baking tray or roasting tin (measuring 33 × 45cm/ 13 × 18in) or two smaller trays, and tip the dough out of the container into the centre (dividing it in half if using two trays). Use your fingers to stretch it as far as you can without it breaking, then cover with a tea towel and leave for 10 minutes to relax before stretching again to fill the whole tin. At this stage, you can place the dough in the fridge for up to 12 hours until you're ready to bake. Alternatively, cover again with a tea towel and leave to rise for another 30 minutes.

5   To make the sauce, heat the olive oil in a small saucepan over a medium heat. Add the garlic and fry, stirring often, for 1–2 minutes until fragrant, then add all the other sauce ingredients and simmer for 8–10 minutes until thickened. Remove from the heat and allow to cool to room temperature.

6   Preheat the oven to 240°C (220°C fan/475°F/gas mark 9). Spread the top of the dough with the tomato sauce, then scatter the torn mozzarella over the top. Cover with a layer of pepperoni, then bake in the centre of the oven for 15–20 minutes, rotating the tray halfway through the cooking time.

7   Use a spatula or palette knife to loosen the edges and check underneath the pizza to make sure the base is golden and crisp, then drizzle with honey. Leave to cool for 5 minutes before slicing and serving while hot and gooey!

A table
of delights

Miso paste, a Japanese seasoning made by fermenting soya beans, may sound like a curious ingredient for a banoffee pie, but it's exactly what is needed to balance this otherwise exceptionally sweet dessert. Think of it like salted caramel, but with rich umami undertones. It's delicious topped with ever-so-slightly bitter walnut chunks and curls of sweet white chocolate.

Miso walnut banoffee pie

Serves 8 ~ Preparation time 25 minutes, plus chilling
Cooking time 5–10 minutes

100g (3½oz) walnuts
250g (9oz) digestive biscuits (I like wholemeal ones for this recipe)
125g (4½oz) salted butter
3 large or 4 small bananas
300ml (10fl oz) double cream
white chocolate curls, to decorate

FOR THE MISO CARAMEL
125g (4½oz) salted butter
125g (4½oz) soft light brown sugar
400g (14oz) can condensed milk
2 tablespoons white miso paste

1 Toast the walnuts in a large, deep-sided frying pan over a medium heat for 2–3 minutes (the pan size will feel excessive for the nuts, but the pan will be used again later in the recipe). Reserve a quarter of the nuts for the topping, and tip the rest into a food processor. Add the digestive biscuits and blitz until finely ground.

2 Melt the butter in the frying pan over a low heat, then pour it into the biscuit crumbs and mix well until completely combined. Press the mixture into the base and up the sides of a 23cm (9in) loose-bottomed tart tin (I use a small glass or cup to help), making sure it is well compacted, then place in the fridge to set for a minimum of 2 hours.

3 To make the miso caramel, add the butter, brown sugar and condensed milk to the now-empty frying pan. Stir over a low heat until the sugar has dissolved and the mixture is bubbling. Add the miso paste and stir to combine, then pour the caramel into the pie crust and return to the fridge for at least 1 hour to set.

4 When you are ready to serve, release the pie from the tin. Slice the bananas lengthways and lay them across the top of the caramel, so they just stick over the edges. In a large bowl, whip the cream to soft peaks – I usually do this by hand, but you can use an electric whisk – then dollop all over the top of the pie. Roughly chop the reserved walnuts, then sprinkle over the top, along with the white chocolate curls. Serve immediately.

Everyone's favourite Italian dessert gets a frozen makeover! Creating a semi-freddo-style base means you can slice this at the table to reveal the layers inside, without the fear of your tiramisu not being set. You can make this dessert up to 2 weeks before you need it and store it in the freezer.

Frozen tiramisu

Serves 8 ~ Preparation time 25 minutes, plus freezing

vegetable oil, for greasing
2 large eggs
75g (2¾oz) caster sugar
1 tablespoon runny honey
250g (9oz) mascarpone
300ml (10fl oz) double cream
1 teaspoon vanilla bean paste
250ml (9fl oz) strong coffee (such as espresso), at room temperature
4 tablespoons marsala wine or coffee liqueur
200g (7oz) sponge fingers
2 tablespoons cocoa powder

FOR THE CHOCOLATE SAUCE
75g (2½oz) dark chocolate
150ml (5fl oz) double cream
pinch of sea salt flakes

1 Brush a 900g (2lb) loaf tin with a small amount of oil, then line with a sheet or two of clingfilm.

2 Separate the eggs, placing the whites in a medium-sized mixing bowl and the yolks in a large mixing bowl or the bowl of a stand mixer.

3 Add the sugar and honey to the egg yolks, then whisk on a high speed using an electric whisk or a stand mixer for 4–5 minutes, until the mixture becomes thick and pale in colour. When you lift out the whisk, it should leave a trail that lasts on the top of the mixture for at least 3 seconds before disappearing.

4 Add the mascarpone, double cream and vanilla to the whisked egg yolks. Whisk for a further 3–4 minutes, until the mixture is thick and billowy.

5 Clean the whisk beaters thoroughly (any fat residue will prevent the whites from whipping), then whisk the egg whites until soft peaks form. Fold the egg whites through the mascarpone mixture until just combined.

6 Stir together the coffee and marsala wine or coffee liqueur in a small, shallow bowl that is large enough to hold a few sponge fingers at a time.

continued overleaf...

165

7. Spread a thin layer of the mascarpone cream over the base of the loaf tin. Dunk each sponge finger into the coffee mixture, submerging each one for no more than 5 seconds, so they absorb enough flavour but don't fall apart. Arrange the fingers in a layer on top of the cream, running parallel with the long side of the tin. Cover with another layer of cream, then repeat the process with the sponge fingers. Finish with the remaining cream, then a final layer of sponge fingers, before wrapping the tin in cling film. Freeze for at least 8 hours, ideally overnight.

8. To make the chocolate sauce, combine the dark chocolate and double cream in a small saucepan and place over a low heat. Stir continuously for 4-5 minutes, or until the chocolate has completely melted and the sauce is smooth. Add a pinch of sea salt flakes, then pour into a small bowl and leave to cool.

9. Remove the frozen tiramisu from the freezer 5 minutes before you want to serve it. Unwrap, then invert on to a plate and remove the clingfilm. Dust generously with cocoa powder and serve slices with a drizzle of chocolate sauce.

TIP
Be sure to use strong coffee and to soak your sponge fingers well so that they absorb enough flavour.

This simple condensed milk fudge is delicious – and so easy to make. The flavour of the coffee mixed with the sweet condensed milk reminds me of Vietnamese coffee. Make sure you use an instant coffee that is nice and intense in flavour to make it punchy, as well as high-quality dark chocolate. If you don't want to make a full batch, you can halve the quantities and use a loaf tin to set this fudge instead.

Coffee and chocolate layered fudge

Makes 64 squares ~ Preparation time: 15 minutes, plus chilling
Cooking time 5–10 minutes

15g (½ oz) salted butter, plus extra for greasing
250g (9oz) dark chocolate (60–70 per cent cocoa solids), finely chopped
400g (14oz) can condensed milk
250g (9oz) white chocolate
2 tablespoons good-quality instant coffee powder
1–2 teaspoons boiling water
2 tablespoons whole coffee beans, to top (optional)

1. Grease a 20cm (8in) square baking tin with butter and line with baking parchment.

2. Fill a saucepan a third full of boiling water, then place over a low heat so it is gently simmering. Place the dark chocolate in a large heatproof bowl, along with the butter and half the condensed milk. Set the bowl over the pan of water, keeping the heat as low as possible and making sure the bowl doesn't come into contact with the water so you don't overheat the chocolate. Stir continuously until the ingredients are melted together and the mixture looks smooth and glossy. Pour into the prepared tin and use a spatula to spread it into an even layer.

3. Take a separate heatproof bowl (or clean the one you just used). Add the white chocolate, along with the remaining condensed milk. In a cup, mix the coffee powder with the measured boiling water to make a thick paste, then add this to the bowl with the chocolate and condensed milk. Place over the pan of simmering water and heat in the same way as before, then pour this mixture over the top of the chocolate layer and spread out evenly.

4. Scatter the coffee beans over the top, if using, pressing them down gently to help them stick. Place the tin in the fridge for at least 3 hours to set before slicing the fudge into cubes. It will keep up for up to 1 month, stored in an airtight container in the fridge.

TIP
If you find your chocolate seizes (becomes grainy) as you melt it, don't worry! You can rescue it by adding a small amount of boiling water, 1 tablespoon at a time, and beating vigorously until it looks smooth and glossy again.

There is something beautiful about the simplicity of a New York cheesecake. Browning the butter for the base is a change that I hope will be acceptable to New Yorkers, as it adds a nutty complexity to the biscuit layer. This dessert sinks or swims depending on the quality of the cream-cheese layer. Mix it gently, bake with care and chill properly before serving for silky-smooth results that everyone will adore.

Brown butter New York cheesecake

Serves 10 ~ Preparation time 15 minutes, plus **chilling**
Cooking time 1 hour 10 minutes–1 hour 15 minutes

FOR THE BASE
75g (2¾oz) salted butter, plus extra for greasing
200g (7oz) digestive biscuits (I like wholemeal ones for this recipe)

FOR THE FILLING
750g (1lb 10oz) full-fat cream cheese
160g (5¾oz) caster sugar
1 teaspoon vanilla bean paste
zest of 1 lemon
1 tablespoon cornflour
4 large eggs
200ml (7fl oz) soured cream

1. Preheat the oven to 180°C (160°C fan/350°F/gas mark 4). Take a deep-sided 23cm (9in) round cake tin with a removable base, and wrap the base piece with a layer of foil, tucking the edges underneath. This will make it much easier to remove the cheesecake from the tin later on. Press the wrapped base back into the tin and grease the sides generously with butter.

2. To make the base, melt the butter in a small saucepan over a medium heat until completely melted. Continue to cook for a few minutes more, swirling the pan often, until the butter starts to foam and smell nutty. Once some of the solids in the butter have turned golden brown, remove the pan from the heat.

3. Add the biscuits to a food processor and blitz to fine crumbs. Stir through the browned butter until coated, then press firmly into the base of the prepared tin. Bake for 10 minutes, then remove from the oven and allow to cool in the tin.

4. Now prepare the filling. In a large bowl (or the bowl of a stand mixer), mix together the cream cheese, sugar, vanilla bean paste, lemon zest and cornflour. Use an electric whisk on the lowest speed or the paddle attachment of the stand mixer, as you don't want to incorporate too much air.

5. Beat the eggs in a small jug, then add the soured cream and mix until smooth.

6. Combine the two mixtures using a spatula until well combined, then leave to sit for a few minutes to allow any bubbles to escape. Tapping the bowl firmly on the work surface a few times will aid this process.

7. Pour the cheesecake mixture on top of the cooled base and spread out in an even layer using a spatula. Place the cake tin on a baking tray to catch any leaks, then transfer to the oven. Bake for 15 minutes, then reduce the oven temperature to 150°C (130°C fan/300°F/gas mark 2) and bake for a further 50–55 minutes. When the cheesecake is ready, it should wobble like a jelly when gently shaken, but it should not look runny. Turn off the oven, leave the door slightly ajar and allow the cheesecake to cool to room temperature while still in the oven.

8. Once cool, remove the cheesecake from the oven and run a palette knife around the inside to loosen it. Chill overnight, or for at least 6 hours, before pushing out of the tin, unfolding the foil and transferring the cheesecake from the sheet of foil to a plate. The cheesecake will keep for up to 3 days in the fridge.

This recipe makes a large bowl, perfect for sharing and decorating with addictive toppings like my salted honeycomb pistachio crunch and a few fresh raspberries! The recipe is easy to scale down if you're cooking for fewer people, and it can also be portioned into individual glasses if you prefer.

Serve–yourself dark chocolate mousse

Serves 8–10 ~ Preparation time 30 minutes, plus chilling
Cooking time 10 minutes

275g (9¾oz) dark chocolate (60–70 per cent cocoa solids), broken into pieces
4 large eggs
65g (2½oz) caster sugar
350ml (12fl oz) double cream

FOR THE SALTED HONEYCOMB PISTACHIO CRUNCH
150g (5½oz) caster sugar
1½ tablespoons runny honey
2 tablespoons water
⅛ teaspoon bicarbonate of soda
pinch of fine sea salt
40g (1½oz) pistachio nuts, roughly chopped
30g (1oz) cornflakes, lightly crushed

TO SERVE
whipped cream
fresh raspberries

1. Place the dark chocolate in a large heatproof bowl set over a saucepan of barely simmering water and allow to melt, stirring occasionally. Once it's melted and smooth, remove from the heat and allow to cool to room temperature.

2. Separate the eggs, placing the whites in a clean mixing bowl and adding the yolk to the bowl of chocolate. Stir to combine (the mixture will thicken considerably – don't worry about this).

3. Using an electric whisk, whip the egg whites until they form soft peaks. Add the caster sugar and briefly whisk again. Add a third of the whisked egg white to the chocolate mixture and stir well. This loosens up the mixture so it is easier to incorporate the rest of the whites without knocking out too much air. Add the remaining whites and carefully fold through in a figure-of-eight motion using a spatula or balloon whisk until no white streaks of egg remain.

4. Pour the double cream into the mixing bowl you used to whisk the egg whites (no need to wash it) and whip to soft peaks using the electric whisk. Fold the whipped cream into the mousse until just combined, being careful not to overmix.

TIP
You can make the salted honeycomb pistachio crunch in advance, but be sure to store it in an airtight container until you're ready to serve, so that it stays crunchy.

continued overleaf...

5   Gently spoon the mousse into a large serving bowl and smooth the top. Chill in the fridge for at least 3 hours to set.

6   To make the salted honeycomb crunch, line a small baking tray with baking parchment. Combine the sugar, honey and measured water in a small saucepan over a medium heat and stir well. Bring to a simmer, then allow to bubble for around 5 minutes, swirling the pan occasionally, until the mixture is a light caramel colour and has a caramel aroma. Remove from the heat and stir in the bicarbonate of soda and the salt – the mixture will bubble and foam. Working quickly, add the pistachios and cornflakes and mix to coat. Tip the mixture into the tray and leave to cool completely (at least 15 minutes) before breaking up into small shards.

7   Remove the mousse from the fridge 20 minutes before serving, then present family-style at the table, allowing guests to serve their own portions into small bowls. Place the honeycomb crunch, raspberries and whipped cream in the centre of the table to use as toppings.

The perfect wobbly treat for a celebration! Swap out the strawberries for cranberries if you're making this during the festive season, or try setting the jelly in small shot glasses for a sweet canapé.

Prosecco jellies

Serves 8 ~ Preparation time 10 minutes, plus chilling
Cooking time 5 minutes

8 sheets of leaf gelatine
100g (3½oz) caster sugar
125ml (4fl oz) water
750ml (3 cups) Prosecco
100g (3½oz) pomegranate seeds
4 strawberries, halved or quartered

1. Fill a small bowl with cold water and add the gelatine sheets. Leave to soak for 5 minutes.

2. Meanwhile, in a small saucepan, combine the sugar with the measured water and 125ml (4fl oz) of the Prosecco. Warm over a low heat, stirring, until the sugar has dissolved, then take off the heat.

3. Squeeze the excess water from the gelatine sheets, then add them to the warm sugar syrup and stir until smooth.

4. Divide the pomegranate seeds and strawberries between 8 glasses, preferably champagne flutes. Stir the remaining Prosecco into the gelatine mixture, then immediately pour it over the fruit. Chill for at least 3 hours or until firmly set. The jellies will keep in the fridge for up to 4 days.

This rustic, free-form tart consisting of homemade flaky pastry enveloping ripe peaches scented with lemon thyme and sweet wine instantly transports you to a sunny day in the south of France. It's best enjoyed with a dollop of Greek yogurt and a chilled glass of dessert wine in hand.

Sweet wine peach galette

Serves 8 ~ Preparation time 30 minutes, plus chilling
Cooking time 40–45 minutes

FOR THE PASTRY
30g (1oz) ground almonds
225g (8oz) plain flour
25g (1oz) caster sugar
150g (5½oz) butter, chilled and cubed
1 egg
4 tablespoons cold water
2 teaspoons demerara sugar

FOR THE FILLING
450g (1lb) ripe peaches or nectarines (about 4), stoned and sliced into wedges
50g (1¾oz) caster sugar
2 tablespoons cornflour
1 teaspoon vanilla bean paste
1 tablespoon Sauternes (or other dessert wine)
a couple of lemon thyme sprigs, leaves picked
2 tablespoons ground almonds

FOR THE GLAZE
1 tablespoon apricot jam
1 tablespoon Sauternes (or other dessert wine)

Greek yogurt, to serve

1 Start by making the pastry. Add the almonds, flour and caster sugar to food processor (or a large mixing bowl) and mix to combine. Add the cubed butter. If using the food processor, pulse a few times, until the butter is in pea-sized pieces. Don't pulse too finely, as you want visible streaks of butter; these will melt in the oven for a flaky pastry. If you're doing this by hand, rub in the butter using your fingers until you have a mix of breadcrumbs and pea-sized chunks.

2 Remove the blade from the food processor, if using. Separate the egg, reserving the white for later, and whisk the egg yolk in a jug with the measured cold water. Add this to the mixture and stir with a round-bladed knife until the dough starts to come together. You may need to add a little more water, but don't overdo it, as you're looking for a fairly dry dough.

3 Squeeze the dough between your hands to make a cohesive ball, then wrap and chill in the fridge for at least 1 hour.

4 Spread a large piece of baking parchment over the worktop and place the chilled pastry in the centre. Roll it out into a large circle, around 30cm (12in) in diameter and around 5mm (¼in) thick – the edges will be a little craggy. Slide the pastry, still on the parchment, on to a large baking sheet, cover loosely, then chill again while you prepare the filling.

5 For the filling, combine the peach wedges in a large mixing bowl with the sugar, cornflour, vanilla bean paste, Sauternes and half the lemon thyme leaves. Mix well and set aside.

continued overleaf...

6   When you're ready to bake, preheat the oven to 190°C (170°C fan/375°F/gas mark 5). Sprinkle the centre of the pastry with the ground almonds. Arrange the fruit in the centre in a single layer, leaving a clear border of 3cm (1¼in) around the edges. Try not to pile the fruit pieces on top of each other, or the resulting tart will be too wet. Leave any excess liquid in the bowl at this point.

7   Create a rim on the galette by using the baking parchment to fold the pastry border up and over the fruit, pressing it around the edges. Repeat all the way around, and don't worry about it being neat – that's the beauty of the galette! Pour any of the liquid remaining the bowl over the exposed fruit. Beat the reserved egg white and brush it over the pastry rim, then sprinkle it with the demerara sugar.

8   Bake the galette for 40–45 minutes, until the pastry is deep golden and crisp all the way around.

9   Warm the apricot jam and sweet wine together in a small saucepan over a low heat, then use a pastry brush to glaze the fruit all over, while it's still hot from the oven. The filling may look runny, but if you allow it to cool to room temperature before slicing, it will thicken and set. Serve with the remaining lemon thyme leaves and a dollop of Greek yogurt.

My mum used to bake a lot of pavlovas when I was growing up, often leaving the meringue base to cool in the oven overnight. I remember many a hairy moment where one of us would unwittingly turn on the oven the next morning, ruining all her hard work as the smell of singed sugar filled the kitchen. I now leave a sticky note on the oven door to avoid such disasters, and recommend you do the same.

Elderflower and strawberry pavlova

Serves 8–10 ~ Preparation time 25 minutes, plus cooling
Cooking time 1 hour 45 minutes

400g (14oz) strawberries, hulled and chopped
2 tablespoons elderflower cordial
juice of ½ lemon
2 teaspoons caster sugar
400ml (14fl oz) double cream
1 mint sprig, leaves picked and chopped

FOR THE MERINGUE
150ml (5fl oz) egg whites (around 5 eggs)
300g (10½oz) caster sugar

1. Begin by making the meringue. Preheat the oven to 120°C (100°C fan/250°F/gas mark ½) and line a large baking tray with baking parchment.

2. In the bowl of a stand mixer or a large bowl if using a hand-held electric whisk, whisk the egg whites until they form stiff peaks.

3. Carefully whisk the sugar into the egg whites, adding a spoonful at a time and ensuring each one is fully incorporated before adding the next. When all the sugar has been added, increase the mixer speed and whisk for 5–6 minutes more, or until the mixture is thick and glossy. If you rub a small amount between your fingers, you shouldn't be able to feel any grains of sugar. If it is still gritty, continue to whisk for a few more minutes until it feels smooth.

4. Spoon the meringue on to the prepared baking tray and heap into a circle about 23cm (9in) in diameter. Use the back of a spoon to drag the edges up, creating pretty ripples. Bake in the centre of the oven for 1 hour 45 minutes, then turn off the oven and allow the meringue to cool completely in the oven before removing.

5. When you're nearly ready to serve, toss the strawberries in a large bowl with the elderflower cordial, lemon juice and sugar until coated, then leave for 10 minutes to macerate.

6. In a separate large bowl, whip the cream to soft peaks, either by hand or using an electric whisk, and spread it on to the cooled pavlova. Top with the strawberries and a few spoonfuls of the juice they will have produced, and scatter over the chopped mint just before serving.

TIP
Use the egg yolks to make the Pastéis de Nata Ice Cream on page 182.

Autumnal and richly coloured, plums are ideal for crumble as they hold their shape just enough, while also yielding a jammy sauce. Floral ground cardamom is a great partner for plums, but you can substitute ground ginger if you don't have any or don't care to grind your own, as this flavour works harmoniously too.

Plum and cardamom crumble

Serves 4 ~ Preparation time 25–30 minutes
Cooking time 30 minutes

FOR THE FILLING
12 ripe plums, stoned and quartered
½ teaspoon ground cinnamon
50g (1¾oz) soft light brown sugar

FOR THE CRUMBLE
175g (6oz) plain flour
150g (5½oz) cold salted butter
75g (2¾oz) soft light brown sugar
50g (1¾oz) oats
seeds from 5 cardamom pods or
 ½ teaspoon ground cardamom

1 Preheat the oven to 200°C (180°C fan/400°F/gas mark 6).

2 Arrange the plum quarters in a medium baking dish (I use a 22cm/8½in round pie dish or a 20cm/8in square dish) and sprinkle with the cinnamon and sugar. Toss well to combine, then set aside.

3 To make the crumble topping, tip the flour into a large bowl and add the butter, rubbing it into the flour with your fingers until it starts to clump together and you can't see any large chunks of butter. Alternatively, use a food processor to pulse the ingredients together. Stir in the sugar and oats, and mix with your hands. Add the cardamom; if using cardamom pods, de-pod the seeds and use a pestle and mortar or spice grinder to grind them to a fine powder, then add to the mixture and stir well.

4 Sprinkle the crumble topping over the plums and bake for 30 minutes, or until golden brown and piping hot. Allow to cool for 5 minutes before serving so the filling can thicken, then serve with ice cream or custard.

Should you ever consider inviting me to holiday with you in Portugal, I can assure you that my response will be an enthusiastic yes. Why, you ask? Custard tarts. For me, a trip to Lisbon means snaffling pastéis de nata at every opportunity. This is my favourite treat turned into ice-cream: a rich custard base flecked with caramelized buttery pastry flakes dusted in sugar and cinnamon, like the tarts themselves.

Pastéis de nata ice cream

Makes 1 litre (4 cups) ~ **Preparation time** 20 minutes, plus chilling and churning ~ **Cooking time** 30–35 minutes

475ml (17fl oz) double cream
250g (9oz) whole milk
125g (4½oz) caster sugar
2 teaspoons vanilla bean paste
¼ teaspoon table salt
6 large egg yolks (see tip)
125g (4½oz) puff pastry (cut from a shop-bought block)
1 tablespoon icing sugar
1 teaspoon ground cinnamon

1. Combine the cream, milk, sugar, vanilla and salt in a large saucepan and heat gently over a low heat until the mixture is steaming and the sugar has dissolved. Remove from the heat.

2. Use a balloon whisk to mix the egg yolks in a measuring jug.

3. Carefully add about a third of the hot cream in the jug with the egg yolks, whisking as you do so, until the mixture is smooth. Add the remaining warm cream mixture, whisk briefly to combine, then pour it all back into the saucepan. Heat over a low heat, stirring all the time, for 8–10 minutes, until the custard is thick enough to coat the back of a wooden spoon or spatula (when you run your finger across the back, it should leave an a clear line without filling in).

4. Once the custard is thick, remove it from the heat and pass through a sieve into the measuring jug. Cover with clingfilm, making sure it is in contact with the surface of the custard to prevent a skin forming, then chill for at least 4 hours until cold.

5. Meanwhile, preheat the oven to 220°C (200°C fan/425°F/gas mark 7) and line a baking tray with baking parchment. Find another baking tray of the same size and set aside. Roll the puff pastry into a thin layer around 5mm (¼in) thick and dust with icing sugar and cinnamon on both sides. Place this on the baking parchment, then cover with another layer of parchment and place the second baking tray on top to compress it.

6   Bake for 20–25 minutes, removing from the oven halfway through to press the top tray down firmly to expel any excess air before returning it to the oven. The pastry should look golden brown and deeply caramelized when you lift the top tray to check. Allow to cool completely before using a serrated knife to slice the pastry into small squares, approximately 2cm (¾in).

7   Churn the cooled custard using an ice-cream maker according to the manufacturer's instructions. Once frozen, spoon a third of the mixture into a freezer-proof container, then sprinkle with a layer of caramelized pastry squares. Repeat with another third of the remaining ice cream and some more pastry squares, gently swirling it together, then top with the remaining ice cream. Press a few pastry squares into the ice cream and sprinkle with the remaining squares, then freeze until solid.

8   Remove the ice cream from the freezer approximately 5 minutes before serving to make it easier to scoop. This will keep for up to 3 months in the freezer.

TIP
Save the egg whites – you can freeze them and then defrost them for a pavlova (see page 178 for mine).

Sticky toffee pudding is arguably the most comforting dessert there is and this recipe takes it to new levels of heartwarming, courtesy of Medjool dates soaked in heady spiced chai, with more aromatic spices mixed into the batter. Other types of tea will also work in this dessert, but chai is by far my favourite for a cosy night in during the winter.

Chai-spiced sticky toffee pudding

Serves 6–8 ~ **Preparation time** 20 minutes
Cooking time 30–35 minutes

100g (3½oz) salted butter, softened, plus extra for greasing
1 chai teabag
165ml (5½fl oz) boiling water
165g (5¾ oz) pitted Medjool dates, finely chopped
1 teaspoon bicarbonate of soda
1 teaspoon vanilla extract
150g (5½oz) dark muscovado sugar
2 large eggs
2 tablespoons golden syrup
175g (6oz) self-raising flour
1 teaspoon ground cinnamon
½ teaspoon ground ginger
5 tablespoons whole milk
vanilla ice cream or custard, to serve

FOR THE TOFFEE SAUCE
225g (8oz) dark muscovado sugar
1 tablespoon golden syrup
100g (3½oz) salted butter
200ml (7fl oz) double cream

1. Preheat the oven to 200°C (180°C fan/400°F/gas mark 6) and grease a 20 x 32cm (8 x 12½in) ovenproof dish with butter. In a small bowl, cover the chai teabag with the measured boiling water and leave to brew for a few minutes. Add the chopped dates, along with the bicarbonate of soda and vanilla extract, then stir to combine. Leave to soak for 20 minutes.

2. In a large bowl, beat the butter and sugar together with a wooden spoon or electric whisk for a few minutes until light and fluffy. Add the eggs, one at a time, beating well between each addition, followed by the golden syrup. Stir in the flour, cinnamon and ginger until incorporated, then pour in the milk and beat well.

3. Remove the teabag from the date mixture, squeezing it against the side of the bowl to extract maximum flavour. Use a fork to mash the dates into a chunky paste, then fold this into the batter.

4. Spread the mixture evenly over the buttered dish and bake for 30–35 minutes until risen, golden and firm.

5. While the pudding is baking, make the toffee sauce. Combine the sugar, golden syrup, butter and cream in a medium saucepan over a medium heat. Bring to the boil, stirring all the time, until the sugar has completely dissolved. Increase the heat slightly and let the mixture bubble for 2–3 minutes until it is a rich toffee colour.

6. Once the pudding is cooked and a skewer inserted into the centre comes out clean, pierce the top in several places using the skewer and pour half the sauce over the top of the pudding. Return the pudding to the oven for 5 minutes to allow the sauce to be absorbed and make the pudding extra sticky.

7. Remove the pudding from the oven and leave to stand for 5 minutes, then serve with the remaining sauce and piping-hot custard or balls of vanilla ice cream!

The perfect end to a meal, especially if you've got an espresso machine! Choose a fruity and full-bodied coffee to complement the flavours of the drunken cherries. These are a pantry staple in my kitcheb: amaretto is my spirit of choice, because its almondy notes make for syrup reminiscent of a Bakewell tart. You can use the cherries straight away, but they improve after being left to soak for at least a week.

Drunken cherry affogato

Serves 6 ~ Preparation time 10 minutes
Cooking time 10 minutes

500ml (18fl oz) tub good-quality vanilla ice cream
300ml (10fl oz) hot espresso (or 50ml/2fl oz per person)
50g (1¾oz) dark chocolate, grated

FOR THE DRUNKEN CHERRIES
175ml (6fl oz) water
80g (2¾oz) caster sugar
500g (1lb 2oz) fresh cherries, pitted
4 tablespoons amaretto (or another richly flavoured spirit like brandy or dark rum)

1. Begin by making the drunken cherries. Combine the water and sugar in a medium-sized saucepan over a low heat, stirring until the sugar has completely dissolved.

2. Tip in the cherries and simmer for 5 minutes, until the cherries are tender but haven't become mushy. Remove from the heat and pour in the amaretto. If you're not planning to use the cherries immediately, decant into a sterilized jar (see page 103) and seal – they will keep for up to 3 months stored in a cool, dark place, and will continue to improve in flavour as they age.

3. When you're ready to serve, scoop generous amounts of vanilla ice cream into small bowls or glasses, before spooning a tablespoon of drunken cherries over each portion. Top with a shot of hot espresso and a sprinkling of grated chocolate, then serve immediately.

Drinks trolley

Also known as a portônica, this gorgeously refreshing aperitif is Portugal's answer to a gin and tonic, but with more pronounced citrus notes and honey undertones. Dry white port is preferable here, as it is crisp and herbaceous, rather than sweet and syrupy. On holiday in Lisbon, I grew rather partial to a chilled glass on balmy evenings. Served with rosemary and orange slices, it's a taste of summer.

Porto tonico

Serves 2 ~ Preparation time 5 minutes

ice cubes
2 orange slices
2 rosemary sprigs
120ml (4fl oz) dry white port (I like Taylor's Chip Dry)
240ml (8½fl oz) tonic water

1. Fill 2 large gin or wine glasses with ice, and nestle an orange slice and rosemary sprig into each.

2. Pour over the white port, followed by the tonic, and mix well before serving immediately.

Roadside lemonade stands are a summer tradition in the United States, but not something you see much in the UK. Which is a pity, because I love homemade lemonade. It's ridiculously simple to make from scratch, and you'll know exactly what's in it, which makes it even better. Increase the sugar if you like a sweeter drink, and mix with still, sparkling or soda water, according to your preference.

Homemade lemonade

Makes 1 large jug (serves 10–12) ~ **Preparation time** 10 minutes
Cooking time 5 minutes

6 unwaxed lemons, plus lemon slices, to serve
150g (5½oz) granulated sugar
400ml (14fl oz) water

TO SERVE
1.5 litres (6¼ cups) still or sparkling water, chilled
ice cubes

1. Use a peeler to peel long strips of zest from the lemons, avoiding the white pith. Add these to a medium-sized saucepan with the sugar and measured water. Place over a medium heat and bring to the boil slowly, stirring to dissolve the sugar.

2. Once the syrup comes to the boil, turn off the heat and add the juice of all 6 lemons. Stir well, then leave to cool completely. Once cool, strain into a sterilized bottle (see page 103) and chill until ready to serve. The mixture will keep keep for up to 1 week stored in the fridge.

3. To serve, mix the lemon mixture with chilled still or sparkling water in a jug, and serve over ice with extra lemon slices, if liked.

A fridge-cold glass of peach iced tea is my summer holiday drink – we all have one, right? This has a sweet, refreshing taste that symbolizes putting your feet up and relaxing in the sun. Make up a large jug, or keep a bottle of the syrup in the fridge and mix yourself a glass whenever you fancy a burst of juicy peach freshness.

Peach and basil iced tea

Serves 4 ~ Preparation time 30 minutes
Cooking time 5–10 minutes

4 English breakfast teabags
  (or loose-leaf equivalent)
1 litre (4 cups) freshly boiled water
ice cubes, to serve

FOR THE SYRUP
3 ripe peaches, plus slices to serve
200g (7oz) granulated sugar
250ml (9fl oz) water
10 basil leaves, plus extra to serve

1 To make the syrup, remove the stones from the peaches and roughly chop the flesh, then scrape into a saucepan – juice, skins and all. Add the sugar and measured water and place the pan over a medium heat. Simmer gently for 5 minutes, stirring often.

2 Use a spoon to squash the peaches so they release as much flavour as possible. Once the sugar has dissolved, remove from the heat and add the basil. Cover and allow to steep for 30 minutes.

3 Strain the peach syrup through a sieve into a sterilized glass bottle (see page 103) and chill. The syrup will keep for up a week stored in the fridge.

4 Put the teabags into a jug and pour over the measured boiled water. Leave to brew to your desired strength (I'd recommend brewing slightly stronger than usual, as cold tea is slightly less intense in flavour than hot tea). Remove the teabags, then cover the jug and chill until needed (it will keep for 2–3 days).

5 To serve, fill 4 tall glasses with ice, peach slices and basil leaves. Mix the syrup with the chilled tea to taste and pour into the glasses. Serve immediately.

This is the perfect pitcher to rustle up on the first warm days of the year, to welcome the sunny afternoons (hopefully!) to come. I use sparkling apple juice for extra fizz, but cloudy apple juice also does the job. If you can, forage yourself some elderflower blossom, wash the sprigs well and use to garnish each glass of this sparkling drink.

Elderflower summer punch pitcher

Serves 6 ~ Preparation time 5 minutes

ice cubes
150ml (5fl oz) elderflower cordial
325ml (11fl oz) gin
750ml (3 cups) chilled sparkling apple juice
250ml (9fl oz) chilled Prosecco
1 cucumber
2 apples, thinly sliced
3 mint sprigs

1. Fill a punchbowl or large jug with ice. Add the elderflower cordial, gin, apple juice and Prosecco, then stir well.
2. Slice or peel the cucumber into thin ribbons, then add these to the bowl, along with the apple slices. Garnish with fresh mint and serve.

Nothing says 'party!' quite like a frozen marg, bursting with zesty fruitiness that's balanced by the citrus-salty rim of the glass. And with the high fruit content, you could *almost* pass this off as a healthy way to celebrate summer.

Mango or cherry frozen margaritas

Serves 2 ~ Preparation time 5 minutes

200g (7oz) frozen pitted black cherries or frozen mango chunks
50ml (2fl oz) tequila
25ml (1fl oz) triple sec
handful of ice cubes
juice of 1 lime, plus lime wedges to serve
1–2 tablespoons agave syrup or honey
sea salt flakes, for the rims

1. Tip the cherries or mango into a blender, along with the tequila, triple sec, ice cubes and lime juice. Blitz well, then add enough agave to sweeten to taste.

2. Tip the salt on to a small plate. Run a wedge of lime around the rims of 2 glasses and then dip them into the salt so it sticks. Divide the contents of the blender between the glasses, garnish each one with another wedge of lime, and enjoy!

TIP
You can easily double or even triple this recipe to provide for a crowd – simply ensure your blender is large enough.

Stirred not shaken, this dreamy cocktail is the margarita's younger sister. Bitter with grapefruit and balanced with candied rhubarb syrup, it is pretty and pink, ideal for brunches or afternoon tea. The syrup can be made up to 5 days in advance and stored in the fridge until you're ready to mix.

Rhubarb paloma

Serves 2 ~ Preparation time 15 minutes
Cooking time 8–10 minutes

ice cubes
120ml (4fl oz) tequila
2 tablespoons lime juice
2 tablespoons grapefruit juice
 (use freshly squeezed)
4 tablespoons rhubarb syrup
 (see below)
120ml (4fl oz) soda water

FOR THE RHUBARB SYRUP (MAKES
 ENOUGH FOR 4–6 DRINKS)
125g (4½oz) rhubarb, chopped into
 2cm (¾in) pieces
50g (1¾oz) caster sugar
150ml (5fl oz) water
1 long strip of pink grapefruit peel

TO SERVE
1 rhubarb stick, peeled into ribbons
lime slices
2 small pink grapefruit wedges

1. Start by making the rhubarb syrup. Combine the chopped rhubarb, sugar, measured water and grapefruit peel in a small saucepan and bring to a simmer over a low heat. Cook, stirring often, for 8–10 minutes, or until the rhubarb is soft and collapsing and the sugar has dissolved.

2. Remove from the heat and pour into a sieve set over a small jug. Stir gently, but don't press too firmly or you'll create a cloudy syrup. Once most of the liquid has been extracted, pour into a sterilized bottle (see page 103) and chill the syrup for a minimum of 3 hours before serving. It will keep for up to 5 days stored in the fridge.

3. To make the cocktail, fill 2 highball glasses with ice. In a jug, mix together the tequila, lime juice, grapefruit juice and rhubarb syrup. Stir well, then divide between the glasses and top up with the soda water. Garnish each glass with rhubarb ribbons, rounds of lime and a thin wedge of grapefruit.

TIP
Add more syrup if you prefer a sweeter drink.

This is the hot chocolate I call upon on a cold winter's night, when I'm ready to curl up on the sofa with a good book, or that I take down to the beach in a Thermos flask on a chilly morning. The spices and treacly maple syrup come together to create a warming blend, with dark chocolate chunks for the ultimate cocoa experience.

Spiced hot chocolate

Serves 2 ~ Preparation time 5 minutes
Cooking time 5 minutes

500ml (18fl oz) whole milk
¼ teaspoon ground cinnamon, plus extra to serve
¼ teaspoon ground ginger
¼ teaspoon grated nutmeg
75g (2¾oz) dark chocolate, finely chopped
1 tablespoon maple syrup, plus extra to taste
whipped cream, to serve (optional)

1   Pour the milk into a small saucepan and add the spices. Warm through over a medium heat until the milk is steaming.

2   When the milk is just about to boil, remove the pan from the heat and stir in the chopped chocolate and the maple syrup. Allow to stand for a minute so the chocolate can melt, then whisk until the mixture is smooth and frothy. Return to a low heat if needed to melt any larger chunks of chocolate.

3   Adjust the sweetness to taste with extra maple syrup, then divide between 2 mugs and top with whipped cream and a dusting of cinnamon. Alternatively, pour into a Thermos and take out on a crisp winter walk for a warming treat!

In Germany, mulled wine is known as Glühwein, which translates as 'glow wine', which I like, as a cup of heavily spiced hot wine really does warm you up from the inside, and the resulting merriness provides that festive glow. Making it yourself rather than relying on shop-bought ready-spiced bottles is both easy and rewarding, plus it makes your home smell wonderful.

Mulled wine

Serves 6 ~ Preparation time 5 minutes
Cooking time 10 minutes, plus steeping

1 bottle (75cl) fruity red wine
3 tablespoons runny honey
1 cinnamon stick
2 star anise
6 cloves
5 cardamom pods
5 black peppercorns
3 bay leaves
2 oranges
5 tablespoon brandy, Grand Marnier or Cointreau (optional)

1. Pour the wine into a large saucepan or casserole dish with a lid (see tip). Add the honey, the whole spices and the bay leaves, then stir well.

2. Using a peeler, peel long strips of zest from 1 orange, avoiding the white pith if possible. Add these to the wine, then squeeze in the juice of the orange (discarding any pips).

3. Heat the wine over a low heat, stirring often, until steaming but not quite boiling. Keep it just below boiling for 10 minutes, then put the lid on and turn off the heat. Don't allow it to boil, as this evaporates a lot of the alcohol.

4. Allow the wine to steep for 30 minutes, so the spices can release their aromatic flavours. This is a good time to taste it. If you feel it needs extra sweetness, add a touch more honey.

5. When you're ready to serve, gently warm the mixture and add the brandy (or other spirit, if using). Slice the remaining orange into rounds, then cut each one in half and add to the wine. Remove the whole spices and bay leaves, if liked, then ladle the wine into heatproof glasses or cups, including a slice of orange in each one.

TIP
A slow cooker comes into its own for mulled wine if you want to get ahead. Put the wine, honey, spices, bay leaves, orange zest and juice into the slow cooker, then heat on low for 1½–2½ hours. Add the orange slices and brandy just before serving.

GLOSSARY OF UK/US TERMS

INGREDIENTS
aubergine – eggplant
beef mince – ground beef
bicarbonate of soda – baking soda
caster sugar – superfine sugar
chickpeas – garbanzo beans
coriander – cilantro
cornflour – cornstarch
courgette – zucchini
digestive biscuits – substitute graham crackers
double cream – heavy cream
golden syrup – substitute corn syrup
icing sugar – confectioners' sugar
king prawns – jumbo shrimp
lamb mince – ground lamb
mangetout – snow peas
pak choi – bok choy
pepper (red/green/yellow) – bell pepper
plain flour – all-purpose flour
rocket – arugula
self-raising flour – self-rising flour
spring onions – scallions
stock – broth
Tenderstem broccoli – broccolini
tomato purée – tomato paste

EQUIPMENT
baking parchment – parchment paper
baking tin – baking pan
cake tin – cake pan
clingfilm – plastic wrap
frying pan – skillet
grill – broiler
kitchen paper – paper towels
muffin tin – muffin pan
roasting tray – roasting pan
sieve – fine mesh strainer

INDEX

almonds
  raspberry almond baked oats 14
aubergines
  moussaka bowls 71
avocado
  crab and avocado eggs Benedict 30–2

bacon
  bacon and buttermilk cornbread 117
  French toast with maple-espresso bacon 28
  sticky date baked camembert 90
bananas
  miso walnut banoffee pie 162
basil
  basil oil 123
  basil pesto 80
  peach and basil iced tea 194
beef
  Café de Paris steak and chips 96–8
  coffee bolognese with homemade pappardelle 152–3
  sticky pomegranate brisket with vermicelli rice 140–2
black pepper fritto misto 138
blackberries
  autumn blackberry blondies 51
blueberry cheesecake pancakes 19
brioche
  buttercream brioche toast 24
  brown butter New York cheesecake 168–9
bulgur wheat
  tabbouleh salad 121

butterbeans
  butterbean and pumpkin pot pies 73
  sweet potato dahl with butterbean parathas 82–4
buttercream brioche toast 24
buttermilk
  bacon and buttermilk cornbread 117

cabbage
  Cheddar and jalapeño slaw 122
capers
  cherry tomato, olive and caper focaccia topping 134
caramel
  walnut banoffee pie 162
  speculoos caramel ice-cream sandwiches 128–9
cardamom
  plum and cardamom crumble 181
carrots
  maple pecan carrot cake loaf 50
  pistachio crusted roasted carrots 151
  za'atar roasted carrot and chickpeas 78
celebration sheet cake 54–5
  homemade sprinkles 55
chai spiced sticky toffee pudding 184
cheese
  cacio e pepe gnocchi 107
  Cheddar and jalapeño slaw 122
  cheese and rocket scones 116
  green shakshuka 29
  hasselback halloumi and orange salad 93

  melon, chilli and mozzarella salad 110
  Mexican street corn (elotes) nachos 62
  sheet-pan pizza 157–8
  spanakopita filo triangles 124
  sticky date baked camembert 90
  stovetop macaroni cheese 80–1
  whipped feta sauce 71
  za'atar, feta and pine nut focaccia topping 134
cheesecake
  blueberry cheesecake pancakes 19
  brown butter New York cheesecake 168–9
cherries
  cherry frozen margaritas 196
  runken cherry affogato 186
chicken
  chicken and mushroom pot pies 72
  chicken and sweetcorn noodle soup 68
  creamy chicken cacciatore 66
  Mum's roast chicken 146
  quick spiced chicken shawarma 78
  shredded chicken fajitas 63
chickpeas
  harissa, sausage and sweet potato oven hash 23
  homemade hummus 76
chillies
  melon, chilli and mozzarella salad 110
  pil pil prawns with orzo 69
  Turkish eggs with parsnip fritters 27

203

chives
  scrambled eggs with smoked salmon and chives 33
chocolate
  chocolate-chunk freezer cookies 38
  coffee and chocolate layered fudge 167
  double chocolate marmalade cookies 36
  flourless fallen chocolate and sesame cake 49
  peanut and pretzel popcorn squares 43
  peppermint chocolate slice 47
  serve-yourself dark chocolate mousse 170–2
  spiced hot chocolate 199
cod
  chorizo and cod paella traybake 60
coffee
  coffee and chocolate layered fudge 167
  coffee bolognese with homemade pappardelle 152–3
  drunken cherry affogato 186
  French toast with maple-espresso bacon 28
  frozen tiramisu 164–6
courgettes
  black pepper fritto misto 138
  courgette and golden garlic malfadine 99
  green shakshuka 29
crab and avocado eggs Benedict 30–2
cream
  frozen tiramisu 164–6
  miso walnut banoffee pie 162
croissants
  hazelnut croissant bake 20
croutons 123

cucumber
  almon tikka skewers with mango kachumber salad 104
dates
  sticky date baked camembert 90
  sticky toffee pudding, chai spiced 184

Earl Grey roast salmon 145
eggs
  crab and avocado eggs Benedict 30–2
  green shakshuka 29
  scrambled eggs with smoked salmon and chives 33
  Turkish eggs with parsnip fritters 27
elderflower and strawberry pavlova 178
elderflower summer punch pitchers 195

fennel
  crispy fennel, orange and garlic porchetta 135–7
flourless fallen chocolate and sesame cake 49
focaccia, overnight 132–4
  focaccia topping ideas 134
French toast with maple-espresso bacon 28
fruit, honey-roasted 18

garlic
  courgette and golden garlic malfadine 99
  crispy fennel, orange and garlic porchetta 135–7
  mushroom and wild garlic spelt tarts 118–20
gnocchi, cacio e pepe 107

grapefruit
  honey-roasted fruit 18
  Greek-style potato salad 126

harissa, sausage and sweet potato oven hash 23
hazelnut croissant bake 20
herby Yorkshire puddings 147
hoisin sausage bake 79
hollandaise sauce 30
  my hollandaise has split! 32
honey-roasted fruit 18
honey syrup buns 44–6
hummus bowls with toppings 76–8
  quick spiced chicken shawarma 78
  za'atar roasted carrot and chickpeas 78

ice cream
  pasteis de nata ice-cream 182–3
  speculoos caramel ice-cream sandwiches 128–9

kimchi and prawn fried rice 85

lamb
  moussaka bowls 71
lemons
  homemade lemonade 191
  lemon drizzle layer cake 40
lentils
  sweet potato dahl with butterbean parathas 82–4
lingonberries
  crispy pork schnitzel with lingonberry sauce 103

mango
  mango frozen margaritas 196
  mango lassie lollies 127
  salmon tikka skewers with mango kachumber salad 104

maple syrup
  French toast with maple-espresso bacon 28
  maple pecan carrot cake loaf 50
marmalade
  double chocolate marmalade cookies 36
melon, chilli and mozzarella salad 110
meringue
  elderflower and strawberry pavlova 178
Mexican street corn (elotes) nachos 62
miso walnut banoffee pie 162
moussaka bowls 71
mushrooms
  chicken and mushroom pot pies 72
  mushroom and wild garlic spelt tarts 118–20
  pulled crispy mushroom udon noodles 100

'nduja carbonara 102
noodles
  chicken and sweetcorn noodle soup 68
  pulled crispy mushroom udon noodles 100
  sticky pomegranate brisket with vermicelli rice 140–2

oats
  peach and raspberry crumble squares 39
  plum and cardamom crumble 181
  raspberry almond baked oats 14
olive oil cake with roasted strawberries 56

olives
  cherry tomato, olive and caper focaccia topping 134
  Greek-style potato salad 126
onions
  crispy onions 80
oranges
  blood orange and poppyseed yogurt muffins 15
  crispy fennel, orange and garlic porchetta 135–7
  hasselback halloumi and orange salad 93
  honey-roasted fruit 18

parathas, butterbean 84
parsnip fritters 27
pasta
  coffee bolognese with homemade pappardelle 152–3
  courgette and golden garlic malfadine 99
  'nduja carbonara 102
  pil pil prawns with orzo 69
  stovetop macaroni cheese 80–1
pasteis de nata ice-cream 182–3
pastry tops for pot pies 73
peaches
  peach and basil iced tea 194
  peach and raspberry crumble squares 39
  sweet wine peach galette 174–7
peanut and pretzel popcorn squares 43
pecan nuts
  maple pecan carrot cake loaf 50
peppermint chocolate slice 47
peppers
  Cheddar and jalapeño slaw 122

Padron peppers 88
red pepper muhammara dip 112
pine nuts
  za'atar, feta and pine nut focaccia topping 134
pineapple
  honey-roasted fruit 18
  pineapple pulled pork tacos 154–6
pistachios
  pistachio crusted roasted carrots 151
  salted honeycomb pistachio crunch 170
pizza, sheet-pan 157–8
plum and cardamom crumble 181
polenta
  bacon and buttermilk cornbread 117
  baked polenta chips 143
pomegranate
  sticky pomegranate brisket with vermicelli rice 140–2
poppyseeds
  blood orange and poppyseed yogurt muffins 15
pork
  crispy fennel, orange and garlic porchetta 135–7
  crispy pork schnitzel with lingonberry sauce 103
  pineapple pulled pork tacos 154–6
  pork larb sausage rolls 113
porto tonico 190
potatoes
  Café de Paris steak and chips 96–8
  Greek-style potato salad 126
  moussaka bowls 71
  potato and rosemary focaccia topping 134
  potato dauphinoise 150

205

prawns
  black pepper fritto misto 138
  kimchi and prawn fried rice 85
  pil pil prawns with orzo 69
pretzels
  peanut and pretzel popcorn squares 43
Prosecco jellies 173
pumpkin
  butterbean and pumpkin pot pies 73

quinoa
  hasselback halloumi and orange salad 93

raspberries
  peach and raspberry crumble squares 39
  raspberry almond baked oats 14
rhubarb paloma 198
rice
  chorizo and cod paella traybake 60
  kimchi and prawn fried rice 85
  sticky pomegranate brisket with vermicelli rice 140–2
rocket
  cheese and rocket scones 116
rosemary
  potato and rosemary focaccia topping 134

salmon
  Earl Grey roast salmon 145
  salmon tikka skewers with mango kachumber salad 104
  scrambled eggs with smoked salmon and chives 33
salt-and-pepper sea bream 94

sausage
  chorizo and cod paella traybake 60
  harissa, sausage and sweet potato oven hash 23
  hoisin sausage bake 79
  'nduja carbonara 102
  pork larb sausage rolls 113
  sheet-pan pizza 157–8
sea bream, salt-and-pepper 94
sesame seeds
  flourless fallen chocolate and sesame cake 49
sheet-pan pizza 157–8
speculoos caramel ice-cream sandwiches 128–9
spelt flour
  mushroom and wild garlic spelt tarts 118–20
spiced hot chocolate 199
spinach
  spanakopita filo triangles 124
squid
  black pepper fritto misto 138
steak
  Café de Paris steak and chips 96–8
sticky toffee pudding, chai spiced 184
strawberries
  elderflower and strawberry pavlova 178
  olive oil cake with roasted strawberries 56
  strawberry sauce 24
sweet potatoes
  harissa, sausage and sweet potato oven hash 23
  sweet potato dahl with butterbean parathas 82–4
sweetcorn
  chicken and sweetcorn noodle soup 68

  Mexican street corn (elotes) nachos 62
tabbouleh salad 121
tea
  chai spiced sticky toffee pudding 184
  peach and basil iced tea 194
tiramisu, frozen 164–6
tomatoes
  cherry tomato, olive and caper focaccia topping 134
  creamy chicken cacciatore 66
  melon, chilli and mozzarella salad 110
  sheet-pan pizza 157–8
  summer tomato soup 123
  Turkish eggs with parsnip fritters 27

walnuts
  miso walnut banoffee pie 162
  red pepper muhammara dip 112
wine
  mulled wine 200
  weet wine peach galette 174–7

yogurt
  blood orange and poppyseed yogurt muffins 15
  mango lassie lollies 127
  Turkish eggs with parsnip fritters 27
Yorkshire puddings, herby 147

za'atar roasted carrot and chickpeas 78
za'atar, feta and pine nut focaccia topping 134

ACKNOWLEDGEMENTS

This final page of the book is a thank you, dedicated to all those who have helped bring it into existence. To say this book has been a labour of love is an understatement, as I wrote the vast majority of it during the later stages of my pregnancy, submitting the final manuscript with my two-week-old son peacefully sleeping on my lap. I truly could not have turned my ideas into reality without the unwavering support of family and friends, and the kindness and patience of the team at Kyle Books.

To Judith Hannam and Joanna Copestick, thank you for commissioning this project and giving me the opportunity to bring to life my vision of a book that celebrates the joy of eating together.

To Isabel Jessop, editor extraordinaire! Thank you for upholding the essence of this book, pulling it all together and coordinating all the many aspects that make it so brilliant. To Alex Stetter, thank you for helping the text flow like a dream. To Claire Rochford, thank you for the stunning design and illustrations that weave this book together.

To the fantastically fun shoot team. Seeing this book come to life was both emotional and enjoyable beyond belief. To India Whiley-Morton, for capturing each dish in your easy-going style, which translates onto every page, dappled with joy. To Nicky Collings, for carrying the vision, bringing the energy and creating beauty through your art direction. To Holly Cowgill, for effortlessly executing each dish to perfection and making the food shine. And to Alice and Eden, for assisting and for all the iced coffees on very warm days. To Tabitha Hawkins, for sourcing the gorgeous props that adorn the tables in this book. Each of you are a ray of sunshine. Thank you for the sea swims, laughter, and for dealing with baby feet in the butter.

To my parents, Chris and Lou. I grew up eating around the table, with family dinners and Sunday lunches always made a priority to spend time together. It's a habit I'm infinitely grateful you instilled in me, and one I intend to continue with my own family for many years to come. Thank you for cheering me on, providing feedback, proofreading and being my inspiration in hospitality.

To Han and Taj, Andy and Lizzie, Bea, Emma, Felicity, Jess, Krissy, Larissa, Ruby, Stephen, Wendy and Izzy, thank you for giving your time to test, taste and provide feedback on the recipes in this book. I truly appreciate each one of you!

To my agent, Claudia Young. What a pleasure it has been to work together for over 10 years! Thank you for your faith in me, your encouragement and the way you manage my work and opportunities. You fill me with confidence I wouldn't have otherwise, and I'm beyond grateful for that.

To Michael, who champions me daily and is the best dad to our little one while I chase these crazy dreams. I promise not to attempt to write a book in my third trimester again! In every moment, you are calm and considered, washing the dishes after long days of testing, managing my time plan and making a constant supply of tea. So grateful to be doing life with you.

To KJ, my whole world. This book is for you – you've tasted all the recipes in utero, and I long for the day I can cook them for you as you grow. Delicious days are ahead, little one.

Finally, I thank God for this opportunity and the series of events that have led me here. I am filled with gratitude and give Him the glory every day. 1 John 4:19